CALM IN THE STORM

Proven Techniques for Managing Anger Effectively

Jonathan Masters

Copyright © 2024 by Jonathan Masters

All rights reserved.

No portion of this book may be reproduced in any form without written permission from the publisher or author, except as permitted by U.S. copyright law.

CONTENTS

1. Introduction — 1
2. Understanding Anger — 4
3. Preparing for Change — 24
4. Mindfulness and Relaxation Techniques — 44
5. Cognitive Behavioral Techniques — 66
6. Emotional Intelligence and Anger — 88
7. Lifestyle Adjustments for Anger Control — 105
8. Anger in Relationships — 124
9. Long-Term Strategies for Anger Management — 145
10. Conclusion — 166

Chapter One
Introduction

In a bustling city not so different from your own lived a man named Alex. By most accounts, he was a kind and compassionate person, well-liked by his friends and respected by his colleagues. Yet, there was a hidden beast within him that even Alex had difficulty acknowledging: unmanaged anger.

Alex's story is not unique. Anger is an emotion that all of us have grappled with at one time or another. But for Alex, it was more than an occasional flare-up. It was a persistent, gnawing presence that affected his relationships, work, and overall well-being. He knew he needed help, but the path to transformation seemed elusive.

Anger, in its many forms, is a prevalent issue that impacts countless individuals and society as a whole. It can manifest as explosive outbursts or simmer silently beneath the surface, eroding the very foundations of our relationships and happiness. In this book, we embark on a journey together that traverses the landscape of anger explores the nuances of its origins, and equips you with the tools and insights to manage it effectively.

While there are many resources on anger management, this book takes a holistic approach that recognizes the interconnectedness of our physical, emotional, and social selves. It's not just about suppressing anger or counting to ten; it's about understanding its roots, transforming it into constructive energy, and fostering healthy relationships.

We'll delve deep into anger's physiological and psychological aspects, unravel common misconceptions, and share enlightening statistics about anger and its far-reaching effects. But we won't stop there. This book goes further, offering a comprehensive roadmap for change that includes mindfulness and relaxation techniques, cognitive behavioral strategies, emotional intelligence, and lifestyle adjustments.

Our goal is to help you manage anger and guide you on a path of personal growth and transformation. You'll learn to recognize your anger triggers, explore the purpose of anger, and distinguish between constructive and destructive anger. Through engaging exercises, real-life stories, and practical guidance, you'll build emotional intelligence, improve your relationships, and discover the profound impact of empathy.

Why have I written this book? Because I believe that within each of us lies the potential for profound change. I've witnessed countless individuals, like Alex, who have embarked on their journey from anger to calmness and emerged stronger, happier, and more fulfilled. I want you to experience that transformation too.

As you read this book, you'll gain valuable insights, develop essential skills, and be inspired by the stories of those who've walked this path before you. You'll discover the benefits of improved relationships, enhanced emotional well-being, and greater control over your life.

This book is not just about managing anger; it's about reclaiming your emotional freedom, nurturing healthier connections, and unlocking your full potential. The journey won't always be easy, but it will be transformative. Together, we'll explore the depths of anger and ascend to the heights of emotional intelligence, resilience, and well-being.

Are you ready to embark on this journey from anger to calmness? If so, let's begin. Your transformation starts now.

Chapter Two
Understanding Anger

Imagine a serene lake on a calm morning, its surface as smooth as glass. Suddenly, a stone is thrown into its center, creating ripples that disrupt the peace. Much like that stone, anger can disturb our minds' tranquility, leaving a trail of unsettled emotions. But why does this happen? What lies beneath these turbulent waves?

I recall a particular summer afternoon spent with my family. We were playing a friendly game of Monopoly, a setting you'd expect to be filled with laughter and light-hearted competition. However, as the game progressed, I noticed my brother's mood changing. The once playful banter turned into clenched jaws and curt replies. It was a simple game, yet the stakes felt inexplicably high. His frustration boiled over as he lost his third property, and he abruptly left the room. Witnessing this transformation left me pondering Why anger arises from such trivial matters? How does it escalate so quickly?

This chapter, "Understanding Anger," delves into these questions. It's crafted to unravel the complexities of anger – a universal emotion we've all grappled with at some point. Here, we explore the multifaceted nature of anger: its physiological roots, psychological triggers, and the wide spectrum of its expression. By understanding the anatomy of anger, we can begin to recognize its onset, comprehend its impact, and learn to navigate its turbulent waters.

The benefits of reading this chapter extend beyond mere knowledge. It's a journey toward self-awareness, a tool for recognizing the early signs of anger, and an opportunity to debunk common myths surrounding this intense emotion. Through this exploration, you'll gain insights into how your personal history shapes your response to anger and how, like my brother during that game of Monopoly, seemingly minor events can trigger disproportionate reactions.

Engaging with this chapter is the first step in transforming your relationship with anger. It's not about eliminating this emotion – that would be both impossible and inadvisable. Anger, after all, has its purpose. It signals boundaries and can fuel positive change. However, unmanaged, it can lead to personal turmoil and strained relationships.

So, as we embark on this journey together, remember the lake and the stone. Our goal is not to prevent the stone from creating ripples but to understand why it was thrown and how to restore calm once it has disturbed the water. This understanding is the foundation upon which we will build effective strategies for managing anger, transforming it from a disruptive force into a constructive one. Let's dive into the depths of anger, not as adversaries but as curious explorers seeking to understand a crucial aspect of our emotional landscape.

The Nature of Anger

Anger is an intense and complicated emotion that has perplexed scientists, researchers, and individuals for centuries. To truly comprehend and manage it effectively, it's crucial that we look deeper into the physiological and psychological components that make it such a strong force in our lives.

Physiological Aspects

Imagine anger as an orchestra, with your body as the stage and your brain as the conductor. When the conductor signals anger, a symphony of physiological changes unfolds:

<u>Fight or Flight Response</u>: Anger is intricately linked to our body's ancient "fight or flight" response—a survival mechanism honed over millennia. When a perceived threat or injustice arises, your brain's amygdala sends a signal to the hypothalamus, triggering the release of stress hormones like adrenaline and cortisol. These hormones prepare your body for action, whether confronting or escaping the threat.

<u>Heart Rate and Muscles</u>: In the throes of anger, you may have noticed your heart pounding, fists clenching, or muscles tensing. This physical response is your body gearing up for conflict—a readiness that stems from our evolutionary past.

<u>Seeing Red</u>: *The phrase "seeing red" when someone is angry isn't just a metaphor. For many, increased blood flow to the skin can cause a flushed complexion, and the experience of heat in the face is not uncommon.

The Brain's Role: Within the intricate architecture of your brain, anger ignites a constellation of regions, including the prefrontal cortex, the amygdala, and the anterior cingulate cortex. These regions work together to orchestrate your emotional responses, decision-making processes, and your ability to resolve conflicts.

Psychological Aspects

Beyond the physiological responses, anger carries a psychological landscape that is equally fascinating:

Emotional Signal: Anger often serves as an emotional signal—a call to action. When you feel anger, it's your mind's way of saying, "Something isn't right here!" Much like a warning light on your car's dashboard, anger alerts you to potential problems that need your attention.

Underlying Vulnerabilities: Beneath anger's fiery surface lie hidden vulnerabilities. It can be a mask for deeper emotions such as fear, hurt, or feelings of powerlessness. Understanding these underlying emotions is pivotal to mastering anger because they provide insight into the root causes of our reactions.

Expressing Anger: Anger can manifest in various forms of expression, ranging from assertive and constructive to aggressive and destructive. Finding a healthy outlet for your anger is essential for maintaining relationships and personal well-being.

Distinguishing Constructive vs. Destructive Anger: It's important to note that not all anger is created equal. Constructive anger can serve as a catalyst for positive change, motivating you to address issues and set boundaries. Destructive anger, on the other hand, can lead to harm, regret, and broken relationships. Learning to differentiate between these two forms is crucial.

Dispelling Common Misconceptions

Before we conclude this exploration of anger's nature, let's debunk a few common misconceptions:

Misconception 1: *Anger is Always Destructive*: While destructive anger exists, not all anger is inherently harmful. Constructive anger can be a driving force for positive change when channeled appropriately.

Misconception 2: *Suppressing Anger is Healthy*: Bottling up anger is unhealthy. Repressed anger can lead to various physical and emotional health issues. It's essential to learn how to express it constructively.

Misconception 3: *Venting Anger is the Solution*: The idea of "letting off steam" through venting is a common myth. However, research shows that venting can actually escalate anger and perpetuate negative emotions.

Understanding Anger in Numbers

To further illustrate the importance of comprehending anger's nature, let's glance at some intriguing statistics:

- According to studies, approximately 8% of people experience chronic, long-term anger issues that significantly impact their daily lives.

- Anger is often linked to various health problems, including high blood pressure, heart disease, and weakened immune function.

- The economic cost of workplace anger and conflict in the United States alone is estimated to be in the billions annually.

By exploring anger's physiological and psychological dimensions, we lay the groundwork for effective anger management techniques that will follow in the chapters ahead. As we navigate this intricate emotional landscape, remember that understanding anger's nature is the first step toward transforming it from a tempestuous storm into a source of inner strength and growth.

Triggers of Anger

Anger can arise in response to various external and internal triggers. Recognizing these triggers is key for effective anger management; we will explore common elements that spark off our reactions, the importance of personal history in shaping responses, as well as self-assessment tools to identify your individual triggers.

Internal Triggers

Internal triggers are those that originate within ourselves, often stemming from our thoughts, emotions, or physical sensations:

1. Frustration: Perhaps one of the most common internal triggers, frustration arises when we face obstacles or challenges that thwart our goals. It's the feeling you get when technology refuses to cooperate or when you're stuck in a never-ending traffic jam.

2. Hurt and Pain: Emotional pain, whether from a recent event or past trauma, can serve as a powerful internal trigger. Unresolved hurt from

past experiences can resurface, intensifying our emotional response to present situations.

3. Fear: Fear can manifest as anger when we perceive a threat to our safety or well-being. It's a natural response designed to protect us, but when misinterpreted, it can fuel unnecessary anger.

4. Injustice: The perception of injustice—whether real or perceived—can trigger anger. It's the feeling of being treated unfairly, overlooked, or disregarded.

External Triggers

External triggers originate from the world around us, often in the form of events, situations, or interactions:

1. Criticism: Criticism, especially when delivered in a harsh or disrespectful manner, can instantly trigger anger. It feels like an attack on our self-esteem and competence.

2. Conflict: Engaging in a heated argument or conflict with someone can be a potent external trigger. A clash of differing viewpoints, values, or goals can quickly escalate emotions.

3. Disruption of Plans: Anger may emerge when meticulously laid plans are disrupted by unforeseen circumstances. It's the feeling of frustration when your well-thought-out agenda goes awry.

4. Loss of Control: Feeling out of control in a situation, whether due to circumstances or another person's actions, can trigger anger. It's the sense that your autonomy is being compromised.

The Influence of Personal History

Our personal history plays a significant role in how we respond to anger triggers. It's as if our past experiences shape the lenses through which we view the world. Here's how personal history influences our anger responses:

1. <u>Childhood Experiences</u>: Our early experiences with anger in our families and upbringing can leave lasting imprints. If we grew up in an environment where anger was expressed aggressively, we might replicate those patterns or avoid anger altogether.

2. <u>Past Traumas</u>: Individuals who have experienced trauma—whether it's abuse, loss, or other deeply distressing events—may be more prone to anger as a protective mechanism. Anger can serve as a shield against further harm or as a way to regain control.

3. <u>Cultural and Societal Norms</u>: Cultural and societal norms regarding anger play a substantial role. In some cultures, the expression of anger is encouraged and seen as healthy, while in others, it may be strongly discouraged or considered taboo.

4. <u>Learned Coping Mechanisms</u>: We develop coping mechanisms to deal with anger over time. Some individuals may have learned healthy ways to process and express anger, while others might have learned to suppress it or turn it inward.

Self-Assessment for Personal Triggers

Identifying your personal anger triggers is a crucial step toward effective anger management. Here are some self-assessment tools and strategies to help you recognize and understand your unique triggers:

1. <u>Journaling</u>: Keeping a journal of your anger episodes can be enlightening. Note the circumstances, the people involved, and your emotional and physical reactions. Over time, patterns may emerge.

2. <u>Self-Reflection</u>: Set aside time for self-reflection. Ask yourself why certain situations or interactions provoke anger. Are there underlying emotions or past experiences that contribute to your response?

3. <u>Seeking Feedback</u>: Trusted friends, family members, or a therapist can provide valuable insight. They may have observed patterns or triggers that you're unaware of.

4. <u>Mindfulness Practice</u>: Mindfulness techniques like meditation and deep breathing can increase your awareness of internal triggers. You can observe your emotions without immediate reaction by staying present in the moment.

5. <u>Professional Guidance</u>: If you find it challenging to identify your triggers independently, seeking the guidance of a mental health professional can be immensely beneficial. They can help you uncover deep-seated triggers and provide strategies for managing them.

Understanding and recognizing your anger triggers is pivotal to mastering this powerful emotion. You gain greater control over your responses by becoming aware of the internal and external factors that set off your anger. As we progress through this journey of understanding anger, remember that self-awareness is the compass that guides us toward a calmer and more empowered self.

The Purpose of Anger

Anger is not just a negative emotion. It has a purpose. We will explore the evolution and personal significance of anger. We will also examine how anger can be used to set boundaries, address underlying issues, and differentiate between constructive and damaging expressions.

The Evolutionary Roots of Anger

Survival Instinct: Anger is deeply rooted in our evolutionary history as a survival instinct. Our ancestors faced numerous threats in their environment, and anger, in its purest form, was a tool for self-preservation. When confronted with danger, anger triggers the fight response, equipping individuals to defend themselves or their group.

Boundary Setting: Anger helped our ancestors establish and defend personal boundaries. In the context of tribal communities, asserting oneself and protecting resources were essential for survival. Anger became a natural way to communicate these boundaries to others.

Energy Mobilization: Anger is an energy mobilization tool. When we feel anger, our bodies prepare for action. Adrenaline surges, muscles tense, and focus sharpen. In ancestral times, this heightened state of readiness was crucial when facing physical threats.

The Personal Purpose of Anger

Beyond its evolutionary role, anger serves personal purposes in our lives:

Signaling Discomfort: Anger often arises as a response to discomfort or distress. It's your mind's way of alerting you to a situation or event that doesn't align with your values, needs, or expectations.

Boundary Setting: In personal relationships, anger remains a boundary-setting mechanism. It communicates your limits and reinforces respect for your rights, values, and well-being.

Highlighting Injustice: Anger can respond to perceived injustice or unfair treatment. It fuels a sense of moral outrage, motivating individuals to address wrongdoing and seek justice.

Anger as a Signal

Anger acts as a signal, much like a smoke alarm in your home. It's not the fire itself but the alert that something requires attention. Here's how anger serves as a signal:

1. Boundary Setting: Anger draws a clear line, indicating where your personal boundaries lie. It communicates that someone has crossed those boundaries or violated your values.

2. Unaddressed Needs: Often, anger arises when our needs are unmet or overlooked. It's a reminder to address those needs and prioritize self-care.

3. Emotional Pain: Anger can mask underlying emotional pain, such as hurt, fear, or sadness. It's a way of expressing that something is deeply troubling you.

4. Injustice Detection: When you witness or experience injustice, anger emerges as a call to action. It propels you to right the wrongs and advocate for fairness.

Constructive vs. Destructive Anger

Not all anger is created equal. Understanding the distinction between constructive and destructive anger is pivotal in managing this emotion effectively:

Constructive Anger:

1. <u>Problem Solving</u>: Constructive anger motivates you to address issues and seek solutions. It's a catalyst for positive change, prompting action rather than reaction.

2. <u>Boundary Reinforcement</u>: It helps maintain healthy boundaries in relationships. Constructive anger communicates your limits, fostering respect and understanding.

3. <u>Self-Advocacy</u>: This form of anger empowers you to stand up for yourself and assert your needs and rights assertively.

4. <u>Emotional Release</u>: It allows for the healthy release of emotional energy, reducing internal tension and promoting emotional well-being.

Destructive Anger:

1. <u>Aggression</u>: Destructive anger often leads to aggressive behavior, whether verbally or physically. It harms relationships and can have legal and personal consequences.

2. <u>Escalation</u>: Instead of problem-solving, destructive anger escalates conflicts and intensifies negative emotions.

3. <u>Regret</u>: Actions driven by destructive anger are frequently regretted afterward, as they often harm oneself or others.

4. Health Implications: Long-term, unmanaged, destructive anger can have severe health consequences, including increased stress, heart problems, and a weakened immune system.

Understanding that anger can be channeled constructively empowers you to utilize this emotion as a force for positive change. By recognizing its evolutionary and personal purposes, embracing it as a signal for necessary action, and distinguishing between constructive and destructive expressions, you embark on a path toward mastering anger and transforming it into a source of growth and empowerment.

The Expression of Anger

As a powerful and universal emotion that can be expressed in many ways, anger is a very potent one. We will examine the many facets of anger, highlighting the differences between passive, assertive, and aggressive styles, while also highlighting the possible consequences.

The Spectrum of Anger Expression

It is as if anger has different intensities and colors. We all express anger in different ways, which reflects our personality, upbringing, and coping mechanisms. Here are some of the ways in which people show their anger.

1. Verbal Expression: Verbal expression involves using words to convey anger. This can range from mild irritation to explosive outbursts. Verbal expressions of anger may include yelling, shouting, name-calling, or using sarcasm.

2. Physical Expression: Some individuals express their anger physically. This can manifest as slamming doors, punching walls, or even

engaging in physical altercations with others. Physical expression can be harmful to oneself and others.

3. <u>Passive-Aggressive Behavior</u>: The passive-aggressive style is indirect and often veiled. Instead of openly expressing anger, individuals may use passive-aggressive tactics like sulking, giving silent treatment, or engaging in subtle sabotage.

4. <u>Withdrawal</u>: Some people cope with anger by withdrawing from the situation or relationship. They may choose not to engage in conflict or communication, leading to emotional distance and avoidance.

5. <u>Suppression</u>: Anger suppression involves bottling up one's anger and not expressing it outwardly. While it may appear calm on the surface, this approach can lead to internal turmoil and long-term negative consequences.

6. <u>Manipulation</u>: Manipulative anger expression is characterized by attempting to control or manipulate others through anger. This can involve guilt-tripping, emotional blackmail, or using anger to get one's way.

Distinguishing Expression Styles

Understanding the differences between passive, aggressive, and assertive anger expression styles is pivotal for effective anger management:

1. **Passive Anger Expression**:

Passive anger expression is characterized by an avoidance of conflict and a suppression of emotions. Here are some key traits:

- Avoidance: Individuals with passive anger expressions often avoid addressing the issues that trigger their anger. They may withdraw from conflicts or remain silent.

- Indirect Communication: Passive individuals may use indirect communication or hint at their anger rather than expressing it directly. This can lead to misunderstandings and unresolved issues.

- Internalization: Passive anger expression often involves internalizing anger, which can lead to stress, resentment, and long-term emotional distress.

- Consequences: While passive anger expression may temporarily avoid conflict, it can lead to unresolved issues, damaged relationships, and personal stress.

2. **Aggressive Anger Expression**:

Aggressive anger expression is characterized by the open and hostile expression of anger. Here are some key traits:

- Hostility: Aggressive individuals openly express their anger in ways that may harm others. This can include shouting, verbal abuse, or even physical violence.

- Dominance: Aggressive anger expression seeks to dominate or intimidate others. It may involve blaming, belittling, or using anger as a means of control.

- Immediate Release: Aggressive expression provides immediate release of anger but often at the expense of others' well-being and relationships.

- Consequences: Aggressive anger expression can lead to damaged relationships, legal consequences, and a cycle of conflict and hostility.

3. Assertive Anger Expression:

Assertive anger expression strikes a balance between passive and aggressive styles. It is characterized by respectful and direct communication of anger. Here are some key traits:

- Open Communication: Assertive individuals express their anger openly and directly. They communicate their feelings and needs without resorting to hostility or avoidance.

- Respectful Tone: Assertive anger expression maintains a respectful tone and avoids personal attacks or blame. It focuses on the issue rather than attacking the person.

- Problem Solving: Assertive expression seeks resolution and problem-solving. It aims to address the underlying issues that trigger anger.

- Consequences: Assertive anger expression fosters healthy communication, conflict resolution, and the potential for improved relationships.

The Consequences of Expression Styles

The way we express anger carries consequences that extend beyond the immediate moment. Here's a closer look at the potential outcomes of each expression style:

- Passive Anger Expression: Passive expression may avoid immediate conflict, but it can lead to unresolved issues, emotional distress, and damaged relationships over time.

- Aggressive Anger Expression: Aggressive expression can harm others, damage relationships, lead to legal consequences, and perpetuate a cycle of hostility and conflict.

- Assertive Anger Expression: Assertive expression promotes healthy communication, conflict resolution, and the potential for improved relationships. It seeks resolution and problem-solving while maintaining respect for all parties involved.

As we navigate the labyrinth of anger expression styles, it becomes evident that assertive expression is the most constructive approach. By mastering assertive communication, you empower yourself to express anger effectively, address underlying issues, and cultivate healthier relationships.

The Cost of Unchecked Anger

Anger is a powerful emotion, and when left unchecked, it can exact a toll that extends far beyond the immediate moment. We'll now delve into the profound costs of unmanaged anger, exploring its impact on personal health, relationships, and professional life.

Personal Health Risks of Chronic Anger

1. Physical Health: Chronic anger takes a toll on the body. The persistent release of stress hormones like cortisol and adrenaline can lead to a range of physical health issues. These may include high blood pressure,

increased risk of heart disease, weakened immune function, and even a heightened susceptibility to chronic illnesses.

2. <u>Mental Health</u>: Unmanaged anger also has profound effects on mental well-being. It can contribute to the development or exacerbation of mental health conditions such as anxiety and depression. Prolonged anger can lead to feelings of hopelessness, isolation, and a diminished quality of life.

3. <u>Emotional Well-being</u>: Constant anger erodes emotional well-being. It can result in persistent feelings of frustration, resentment, and hostility. These emotions affect one's mental health and seep into other areas of life, hindering joy and contentment.

4. <u>Relationships</u>: Chronic anger strains relationships with family, friends, and colleagues. It creates an environment of tension and conflict, making it challenging to maintain meaningful connections. The breakdown of trust and communication further deepens the emotional toll.

5. <u>Coping Mechanisms</u>: Individuals grappling with unmanaged anger often resort to unhealthy coping mechanisms. They may turn to substance abuse, overeating, or other forms of self-destructive behavior as an outlet for their anger, compounding the health risks.

Impact on Relationships

1. <u>Family Dynamics</u>: Unchecked anger within a family can disrupt the harmony of the household. It can lead to arguments, emotional distance, and even estrangement among family members. Children exposed to chronic anger may experience emotional trauma with long-lasting effects.

2. <u>Friendships</u>: Friendships often suffer when one or more individuals grapple with unmanaged anger. The inability to communicate effectively or handle conflict can strain even the closest of bonds.

3. <u>Romantic Relationships</u>: Chronic anger can be particularly damaging in romantic partnerships. It erodes intimacy, trust, and emotional connection. Unresolved anger can lead to separation or divorce in extreme cases.

4. <u>Professional Life</u>: Anger in the workplace can have dire consequences. It can strain colleague relationships, hinder teamwork, and impede career advancement. Employees with unresolved anger may find themselves isolated or facing disciplinary actions.

Real-Life Case Studies

<u>Case Study 1</u>: Sarah's Struggle with Chronic Anger

Sarah, a 35-year-old marketing manager, had always struggled with anger issues. Her inability to manage anger effectively had a significant impact on her personal and professional life. She frequently clashed with coworkers and superiors, resulting in a negative work environment. Sarah's anger also strained her marriage, leading to constant arguments and emotional distance. She sought therapy to address her anger issues and learned techniques for managing anger constructively. Over time, her relationships improved, and her career saw a positive turnaround.

<u>Case Study 2</u>: John's Battle with Health Consequences

John, a 45-year-old executive, had a high-pressure job that often left him feeling stressed and irritable. He regularly vented his anger through unhealthy habits, including excessive drinking and poor dietary choices. As a result, his physical health began to deteriorate. He was diagnosed with high blood pressure and developed a heart condition. Recognizing the severe toll his anger was taking on his health, John enrolled in anger management classes and adopted healthier coping strategies. His physical health improved, and he achieved a better work-life balance.

<u>Case Study 3</u>: Emma's Strained Relationships

Emma, a 28-year-old teacher, had a history of explosive anger episodes. Her anger issues led to conflicts with her colleagues, strained friendships, and an unstable romantic relationship. Emma decided to seek therapy to address her anger and learn healthier ways to express herself. Through therapy, she uncovered underlying emotional pain and trauma that fueled her anger. Emma rebuilt her relationships and found greater emotional stability by addressing these issues and learning effective anger management techniques.

Unchecked anger exacts a profound toll on our lives, affecting our physical health, mental well-being, relationships, and professional success. Real-life case studies illustrate the far-reaching consequences of unmanaged anger but highlight the potential for transformation and healing through effective anger management. As we journey through this book, we'll explore strategies and techniques to help you gain control over anger, reduce its negative impact, and cultivate a more balanced and fulfilling life.

Chapter Three

PREPARING FOR CHANGE

Let's embark on a journey through my own experiences—a journey that might strike a chord with many of you. Several years ago, I grappled with anger, much like the woman we'll come to know in this chapter. I was a young professional at that time, navigating the complex landscape of work, relationships, and life's daily stresses.

Beneath the façade of a seemingly well-ordered life, anger was my constant companion. It emerged during heated arguments with loved ones or in moments of overwhelming frustration. I came to realize that this anger not only strained my relationships but also took a toll on my overall well-being.

Recognizing the pressing need for change, I embarked on a journey of transformation—an exploration that would equip me to comprehend and manage anger effectively. While the path was far from easy, it was immensely rewarding. This chapter, "Preparing for Change," holds the keys to establishing the foundation for that transformation.

This chapter lays the groundwork for your personal voyage toward mastering anger management and unearthing inner tranquility.

Before diving into the practical techniques and strategies that will empower you to tame anger, we must establish a sturdy foundation. This chapter serves as your starting point—a bridge that connects your current state to the future you aspire to achieve.

The journey of anger management is not just about suppressing outbursts or bottling up emotions. It's about understanding the nature of anger, its triggers, and how it fits into the broader landscape of your life. The insights gained in this chapter will help you manage anger effectively and promote personal growth, foster healthier relationships, and lead to lasting contentment.

So, why does this chapter matter? It matters because it equips you with the knowledge and self-awareness necessary to navigate the path ahead. It offers you the tools to build a solid emotional infrastructure, allowing you to harness the power of your emotions rather than being controlled by them. As we progress through this chapter, you'll discover the benefits of preparation, laying the groundwork for a more peaceful, fulfilling, and harmonious life.

Accepting Anger

In the pursuit of mastering anger management, our journey begins with a pivotal step—acceptance. It might sound counterintuitive, especially when anger is often seen as something to be controlled or suppressed. But as we delve deeper, you'll discover why acceptance is the foundation for effective anger management.

The Importance of Accepting Anger Without Judgment

One common misconception about anger management is that it's about entirely banishing anger from our lives. However, this view oversimplifies the complex world of human emotions. Anger, like any emotion, is a natural response to certain situations. It's neither good nor bad; it simply is.

Imagine anger as a messenger, a signal from your mind and body that something in your world needs attention. Just as we wouldn't shoot the messenger who brings us important news, we shouldn't judge or condemn anger itself.

Accepting anger without judgment means acknowledging its presence, understanding its message, and responding to it in a healthy and constructive manner. This shift in perspective is vital because it paves the way for a more mindful approach to anger management.

The Role of Mindfulness in Anger Management

Mindfulness—a term that has gained significant popularity in recent years—is a practice deeply intertwined with the concept of accepting anger. At its core, mindfulness involves being fully present in the moment, observing your thoughts and feelings without judgment.

In the context of anger management, mindfulness allows you to become more aware of your anger as it arises. Instead of reacting impulsively, you create a space between the trigger and your response. This space is where transformation happens.

Mindfulness enables you to:

- <u>Recognize Early Signs</u>: By practicing mindfulness, you can identify the early signs of anger, often before it escalates to a full-blown emotional reaction. These signs may include physical sensations like increased heart rate, muscle tension, or a sensation of heat rising within you.

- <u>Gain Clarity</u>: Mindfulness allows you to gain clarity about the source of your anger. Is it rooted in a current situation, or does it connect to past experiences or unresolved emotions? This insight is crucial for effective anger management.

- <u>Choose Your Response</u>: Armed with awareness, you can choose how to respond to anger. You're no longer a slave to impulsive reactions; instead, you become the master of your responses. This newfound control empowers you to select healthier ways of addressing anger.

Exercises for Becoming Aware of Anger Without Acting on It

To embark on the path of accepting anger and integrating mindfulness into your life, consider these exercises:

<u>Breath Awareness</u>: Find a quiet space, sit comfortably, and close your eyes. Take a few deep breaths, focusing your attention on the sensation of the breath entering and leaving your body. When you feel centered, consider a recent situation that triggered anger. Without judgment, observe how your body responds to this memory. Is there tension? Heat? Racing thoughts? Simply notice these sensations without trying to change them. This exercise helps you become more attuned to your physical and emotional responses to anger.

<u>Journaling</u>: Keep a journal dedicated to your anger experiences. When you feel anger rising, jot down your circumstances, emotions, and any

physical sensations you notice. Over time, this journal can help you identify patterns and triggers.

<u>Anger Countdown</u>: Try the "anger countdown" technique when you sense anger building. Mentally count down from ten to one, taking a deep breath with each count. This exercise provides a brief pause that can prevent impulsive reactions.

<u>Mindful Meditation</u>: Set aside time each day for a mindfulness meditation practice. There are various guided meditations available that focus specifically on anger management. These can be valuable tools for enhancing your mindfulness skills.

By consistently engaging in these exercises, you'll cultivate the art of accepting anger without judgment and integrate mindfulness into your daily life. This is a significant step toward mastering anger management and ultimately achieving a more balanced and harmonious existence.

As we continue our journey through this chapter, we'll explore further aspects of preparing for change, including the importance of commitment, building a support system, understanding your anger style, and the role of self-care in your transformation. Each of these components uniquely empowers you to manage anger effectively and embark on a path toward inner calm.

Commitment to Change

Welcome to the second leg of our journey toward mastering anger management—Commitment to Change. By now, you've taken your first steps in understanding anger and accepting it without judgment.

Now, it's time to dive deeper into what it takes to make lasting changes in how you manage your anger.

The Importance of Commitment in Changing Anger Patterns

Imagine you're embarking on a physical fitness journey to become healthier and stronger. You must commit to a regular exercise regimen, watch your diet, and make lifestyle adjustments to succeed. Similarly, mastering anger management is a transformational journey that demands your commitment and dedication.

Why is commitment crucial? Because change isn't a passive process. It requires a proactive, intentional effort to replace old, ineffective anger patterns with healthier, more constructive ones. Without a genuine commitment to change, it's all too easy to slip back into familiar but unhelpful ways of dealing with anger.

Strategies to Strengthen, Resolve, and Set Realistic Goals

Building a strong foundation for anger management begins with strengthening your commitment. Here are some strategies to help you stay resolute on your path to change:

<u>Identify Your "Why"</u>: Begin by understanding why you want to change your anger patterns. Is it to improve your relationships, enhance your well-being, or lead a more fulfilling life? Knowing your "why" will serve as a powerful motivator.

<u>Set SMART Goals</u>: SMART goals are Specific, Measurable, Achievable, Relevant, and Time-bound. Instead of vague intentions like "I want to be less angry," set specific goals such as "I will practice deep breathing exercises for five minutes every morning to manage my anger."

Break Goals into Small Steps: Large goals can be overwhelming. Break them down into smaller, manageable steps. For instance, if your goal is to improve communication during arguments, your first step might be to practice active listening skills.

Create a Vision Board: Visual representations of your goals can serve as daily reminders of your commitment. Use images, quotes, or symbols that resonate with your desire for change.

Find an Accountability Partner: Share your goals with a trusted friend or family member who can offer support and hold you accountable. Sometimes, knowing that someone is cheering you on can make a world of difference.

Track Your Progress: Use a journal or app to monitor your progress. Celebrate your achievements, no matter how small, as they signal steps toward your ultimate goal.

Reevaluate and Adjust: Periodically assess your goals and strategies. Are they working for you? If not, be willing to adapt and refine your approach.

Creating a Personal Plan for Anger Management

Now that you're committed and armed with SMART goals, it's time to create a personalized plan for anger management. This plan will serve as your roadmap, guiding you through the challenges and victories on your journey.

Step 1: Self-Assessment: Conduct a thorough self-assessment of your anger patterns. Reflect on past situations where anger arose, your typical responses, and the triggers that set you off. Understanding your unique anger profile is essential for developing effective strategies.

Step 2: <u>Identify Triggers</u>: Building on your self-assessment, identify your anger triggers—both internal and external. Internal triggers might include stress, fatigue, or certain thoughts, while external triggers could be specific people, situations, or events.

Step 3: <u>Choose Techniques</u>: Explore various anger management techniques and select those that resonate with you. This could include deep breathing exercises, progressive muscle relaxation, meditation, or cognitive-behavioral strategies.

Step 4: <u>Create a Toolbox</u>: Assemble your chosen techniques into an anger management toolbox. Think of this toolbox as your go-to resource when anger strikes. Having various tools at your disposal allows you to select the most appropriate one for any given situation.

Step 5: <u>Practice and Persistence</u>: Begin implementing your chosen techniques in real-life situations. Remember, change takes time and persistence. It's perfectly normal to encounter setbacks along the way. What matters is your commitment to keeping at it.

Step 6: <u>Seek Support</u>: Don't hesitate to seek support when needed. Whether it's from friends, family, or a therapist, having a support system can provide invaluable encouragement and guidance.

Step 7: <u>Monitor and Adjust</u>: Regularly evaluate your progress. Are you seeing improvements in how you handle anger? Are your chosen techniques effective? Adjust your plan as necessary to align with your evolving needs and circumstances.

By following these steps and crafting a personalized plan, you'll be better equipped to navigate anger management challenges. Remember, commitment is the driving force behind lasting change. As you continue your journey, you'll find that your commitment to yourself is a wellspring of strength, propelling you toward a calmer, more balanced life.

Building a Support System

As we continue our journey toward mastering anger management, we arrive at a crucial juncture—creating a robust support system. Just as a ship relies on its crew to navigate tumultuous waters, you, too will benefit from a support network that can guide and sustain you on your path to effective anger management.

Enlisting Help from Friends, Family, or Professionals

Support often begins with those closest to you—friends and family. However, sharing your struggles with anger can be challenging. You might fear judgment, misunderstanding, or even rejection. It's essential to approach this process thoughtfully and strategically.

Here's how to enlist help from your inner circle:

<u>Choose the Right Time and Place</u>: Select a comfortable and private setting for discussing your anger management journey. Timing matters, too; aim for a moment when everyone is relaxed and open to conversation.

<u>Be Honest and Open</u>: Share your experiences and emotions honestly. Let your loved ones know why you're pursuing anger management and how it will benefit you and your relationships.

Listen Actively: Encourage open dialogue by listening to their thoughts and concerns. Remember that they may have their perspectives on your anger patterns.

Set Clear Expectations: Clearly communicate what you need from them. Whether it's patience, understanding, or specific forms of support, being transparent about your expectations fosters mutual understanding.

Seek Professional Guidance: In some cases, involving a therapist or counselor in the conversation may be beneficial. These professionals can provide insights and facilitate productive discussions.

Remember that not everyone in your support system will respond the same way. Some may offer immediate support, while others might need time to process and adjust. Patience and understanding are key as you navigate these conversations.

Tips for Communicating Needs to Your Support System

Effective communication is the linchpin of any successful support system. Here are some tips for articulating your needs:

Use "I" Statements: Frame your requests using "I" statements to express your feelings and needs without placing blame. For example, say, "I feel overwhelmed when arguments get heated, and I need a calmer environment to discuss issues."

Be Specific: Clearly outline what you need from your support system. Whether it's a listening ear, a distraction during tense moments, or reminders to practice anger management techniques, specificity facilitates understanding.

Practice Active Listening: Encourage open communication by actively listening to your support system's thoughts and concerns. This reciprocal exchange fosters empathy and understanding.

Respect Boundaries: Understand that your loved ones may have their boundaries and limitations. Respect their needs, just as you expect them to respect yours.

Express Gratitude: Don't forget to express gratitude for their support. A simple "thank you" can go a long way in strengthening your relationships.

The Role of Support Groups and Community Resources

In addition to your close-knit circle, consider the invaluable resource of support groups and community resources. These external sources can provide unique insights, encouragement, and a sense of belonging.

Support Groups: Anger management support groups consist of individuals who, like you, are on a journey of self-improvement. Participating in these groups offers several benefits:

Shared Experiences: You'll connect with people who understand the challenges of anger management firsthand, reducing feelings of isolation.

Diverse Perspectives: Support groups bring together individuals from various backgrounds, offering diverse perspectives and coping strategies.

Accountability: Regular meetings provide a sense of accountability, motivating you to stay committed to your anger management goals.

Skill Building: Many support groups incorporate skill-building exercises and techniques that complement your journey.

Community Resources: Community resources, such as local counseling services, workshops, or online forums, offer additional avenues for support. They provide access to professionals and information that can enhance your anger management toolkit.

Building a support system is not a one-time effort but an ongoing process. Regularly engage with your support network, maintain open communication, and be receptive to their feedback and encouragement. Together, you can navigate the waters of anger management with greater ease and resilience.

Understanding Your Anger Style

As we delve deeper into the process of preparing for change on your journey to mastering anger management, it's crucial to explore a critical aspect of your relationship with anger—your unique anger style. Just as each person is unique, so too are our approaches to expressing and managing anger. Understanding your anger style is a pivotal step toward achieving lasting transformation.

Identifying Your Anger Style

To begin this exploration, let's embark on a journey of self-discovery by identifying your predominant anger style. Please take a moment to answer the following questions honestly:

How do you typically react when you feel angry?

a) I tend to keep my anger to myself and avoid confrontation.

b) I express my anger openly and directly.

c) I often withdraw and become silent when angry.

d) I use sarcasm and humor to mask my anger.

What physical sensations do you experience when angry?

a) I feel a tightening in my chest or stomach.

b) My heart races, and I may feel a surge of energy.

c) I feel drained and fatigued.

d) I often don't notice physical sensations when angry.

How do you communicate when angry?

a) I tend to avoid discussing my anger and may use passive-aggressive behaviors.

b) I speak assertively, expressing my feelings and needs clearly.

c) I often shut down and refuse to communicate.

d) I resort to sarcasm or jokes to deflect from the issue.

What is your typical response when someone else is angry with you?

a) I become defensive and avoid addressing the issue.

b) I listen to their perspective and try to find a resolution.

c) I withdraw and avoid the person.

d) I may use humor to diffuse the tension.

How do you feel after expressing anger?

a) I feel guilty and regretful.

b) I feel relieved and assertive.

c) I feel emotionally drained.

d) I feel a mix of emotions, including amusement.

Understanding Your Anger Style

Now that you've completed the questionnaire, let's explore the characteristics and implications of each anger style:

a) Passive Anger:

Characteristics: Passive anger is often characterized by suppression of anger, avoidance of conflict, and indirect expressions of displeasure. People with this style may use passive-aggressive behaviors, such as sulking, procrastinating, or making subtle, sarcastic remarks.

Pros: Passive anger may avoid immediate confrontations and maintain a facade of calm. It can be a coping mechanism for those who fear conflict.

Cons: The cons of passive anger include a lack of assertiveness, unresolved issues, and potential damage to relationships due to unexpressed feelings.

b) Assertive Anger:

Characteristics: Assertive anger involves direct and clear expressions of anger while respecting the rights and boundaries of others. People with this style express their feelings and needs assertively and communicate their boundaries effectively.

Pros: Assertive anger promotes open communication, conflict resolution, and the preservation of self-respect. It often leads to healthier relationships.

Cons: The only potential downside is that those unfamiliar with assertive communication may perceive it as aggressive. However, with practice, this misperception can be addressed.

c) <u>Passive-Aggressive Anger</u>:

Characteristics: Passive-aggressive anger combines the avoidance of confrontation with indirect expressions of anger. It may involve behaviors such as procrastination, sarcasm, or subtle sabotage.

Pros: Passive-aggressive individuals may feel a temporary release of anger without engaging in direct conflict.

Cons: This style can lead to misunderstandings, damaged relationships, and unresolved issues. Passive-aggressive behaviors can be hurtful and counterproductive.

d) <u>Humor as a Defense Mechanism</u>:

Characteristics: Some individuals use humor as a defense mechanism to deflect from their anger. They may make jokes or use sarcasm to lighten the mood during tense situations.

Pros: Humor can diffuse tension momentarily and temporarily release anger.

Cons: While humor can be a coping strategy, it may not effectively address the root causes of anger. Over-reliance on humor can also hinder open and honest communication.

Shifting to a More Effective Anger Style

Understanding your predominant anger style is the first step toward transformation. To shift to a more effective anger style, consider the following strategies:

Self-Awareness: Acknowledge your current anger style and its pros and cons. Recognize how it may impact your relationships and overall well-being.

Practice Assertiveness: If you tend toward passive anger, practice assertive communication. Express your feelings and needs directly and respectfully, avoiding passive-aggressive behaviors.

Seek Support: Engage with a therapist or counselor to explore the underlying causes of your anger style and develop healthier coping strategies.

Mindfulness: Practice mindfulness to become more aware of your anger triggers and responses. Mindfulness can help you pause and choose a more constructive reaction.

Learn Conflict Resolution: Develop skills in conflict resolution to address issues openly and find mutually satisfactory solutions.

Remember that shifting your anger style takes time and effort. Be patient with yourself and seek support when needed. Mastering your anger style will pave the way for healthier relationships and greater emotional well-being.

The Role of Self-Care

As we continue to prepare for mastering anger management, it's essential to underscore self-care's vital role in this transformation. Your emotional well-being is intrinsically linked to your physical health and your ability to manage stress effectively. We'll explore how nurturing your physical and emotional well-being through self-care can be a powerful tool in your anger management arsenal.

The Connection between Physical Health and Emotional Well-being

Have you ever noticed how your physical well-being can greatly influence your emotional state? The connection between the body and mind is a profound one. When your physical health is neglected, it can lead to heightened stress levels, increased irritability, and a reduced capacity to manage anger constructively.

Balanced Diet: Fueling Your Emotional Resilience

A well-balanced diet is the cornerstone of physical and emotional health. The foods you consume directly impact your energy levels, mood, and overall well-being. Consider these dietary tips to support your emotional resilience:

Stay Hydrated: Dehydration can lead to fatigue and irritability. Ensure you drink an adequate amount of water throughout the day.

Nutrient-Rich Foods: Incorporate a variety of fruits, vegetables, lean proteins, and whole grains into your diet. These foods provide essential vitamins and minerals that support emotional well-being.

Omega-3 Fatty Acids: Foods rich in omega-3 fatty acids, such as salmon, walnuts, and flaxseeds, have been shown to have mood-stabilizing properties.

Limit Sugar and Caffeine: Excessive sugar and caffeine intake can lead to energy crashes and mood swings. Consume these in moderation.

Mindful Eating: Practice mindful eating by savoring each bite and paying attention to your body's hunger and fullness cues. This can help prevent emotional eating.

Regular Exercise: Energizing Your Mind and Body

Exercise is beneficial for your physical health and plays a significant role in managing emotions, including anger. Here's how regular physical activity contributes to emotional well-being:

Stress Reduction: Exercise triggers the release of endorphins, which are natural mood lifters. Regular physical activity helps reduce stress, anxiety, and depression.

Improved Sleep: Exercise promotes better sleep quality, improving emotional regulation. Aim for at least 30 minutes of moderate exercise most days of the week.

Emotional Release: Engaging in physical activities like jogging, swimming, or kickboxing can provide a healthy outlet for pent-up anger and frustration.

Enhanced Self-Esteem: Achieving fitness goals can boost self-esteem and self-confidence, which can, in turn, reduce feelings of anger.

Adequate Sleep: Recharging Your Emotional Batteries

Quality sleep is essential for emotional well-being and anger management. Sleep deprivation can lead to heightened irritability, decreased impulse control, and a reduced ability to cope with stress. Consider the following tips for improving your sleep patterns:

<u>Establish a Sleep Routine</u>: Go to bed and wake up at the same times every day, even on weekends. Consistency helps regulate your body's internal clock.

<u>Create a Relaxing Bedtime Routine</u>: Engage in calming activities before bed, such as reading, taking a warm bath, or practicing relaxation exercises.

<u>Optimize Sleep Environment</u>: Ensure your bedroom is conducive to sleep by keeping it dark, quiet, and cool. Invest in a comfortable mattress and pillows.

<u>Limit Screen Time</u>: Avoid screens (phones, tablets, computers, TVs) at least an hour before bedtime, as the blue light emitted can interfere with sleep.

<u>Watch Your Diet</u>: Avoid heavy meals, caffeine, and alcohol close to bedtime, as they can disrupt sleep.

Stress Reduction Techniques: Calming Your Emotional Storm

Stress is a significant contributor to anger and can exacerbate your anger response. Learning to manage stress effectively is a vital component of anger management. Here are some stress reduction techniques to consider:

Mindfulness Meditation: Mindfulness practices, such as meditation and deep breathing exercises, can help you stay present, reduce stress, and enhance emotional regulation.

Yoga and Tai Chi: These mind-body practices combine physical postures, movement, and relaxation techniques to reduce stress and promote emotional well-being.

Journaling: Keeping a journal can provide an outlet for expressing and processing emotions. It also allows you to track anger triggers and patterns.

Progressive Muscle Relaxation: This technique involves tensing and relaxing muscle groups to release physical tension and reduce stress.

Hobbies and Leisure Activities: Engaging in hobbies and leisure activities you enjoy can provide an escape from stress and help you relax.

Remember that self-care is not a luxury but necessary for maintaining emotional well-being and effectively managing anger. Prioritizing your physical health, incorporating regular exercise, getting adequate sleep, and practicing stress reduction techniques are powerful tools that will equip you for the journey ahead.

Chapter Four
Mindfulness and Relaxation Techniques

As we embark on this chapter, I want to take you on a journey – a journey deep into the realm of mindfulness and relaxation. Picture yourself in a serene garden, surrounded by the gentle rustling of leaves, the melodious chirping of birds, and the warm embrace of a gentle breeze. In this tranquil setting, I'd like to introduce you to the powerful tools and techniques that await you in this chapter.

But before we dive into the world of mindfulness and relaxation, let me share a story with you that unveils the essence of why this chapter is an indispensable part of our quest for mastering anger management.

Imagine a time when anger was a relentless storm within me. Every setback, every provocation, and every frustration would ignite a tempest of emotions that I struggled to control. Anger would surge through my veins, rendering my rational thoughts powerless. It was as though I were trapped in a turbulent sea with no lifeline.

One fateful day, I had an epiphany while sitting in a crowded coffee shop. I was irritated by the chatter around me, the clinking of cups, and the cacophony of life's daily hustle and bustle. My anger was brewing like a storm cloud, ready to unleash its fury. Something remarkable happened just as I felt on the brink of an explosive outburst.

A soft, soothing melody began to play from the coffee shop's speakers – a tranquil composition of gentle waves lapping against the shore. The melody was accompanied by a calming voice, guiding the patrons through a brief mindfulness exercise. It was as if a lifeline had been thrown to me in the midst of the tempest.

Something extraordinary occurred as I closed my eyes and allowed the soothing sounds and words to wash over me. My anger didn't disappear miraculously, but it lost its grip on me. In that moment of mindfulness, I gained a sliver of clarity and control over my emotions. It was the spark of transformation I had yearned for.

The experience left an indelible mark on me, igniting a fervent curiosity about mindfulness and relaxation techniques. It was a turning point, a beacon of hope that there were tools to navigate the turbulent waters of anger. This chapter exists because I want to share these tools with you.

Now, you might be wondering, "Why mindfulness and relaxation? How can they possibly help me manage anger?" Well, let me assure you, these techniques have the potential to be your staunchest allies on this journey. Here's what you can expect to gain from delving into this chapter:

- Immediate Anger Diffusion: You'll discover practical breathing exercises that can defuse anger in the heat of the moment. Imagine having the power to calm the storm within you at will.

- Emotional Resilience: Mindfulness and relaxation techniques will equip you with the tools to withstand emotional turbulence and maintain composure, even in challenging situations.

- Enhanced Self-Awareness: By practicing mindfulness, you'll better understand your anger triggers and patterns, paving the way for lasting transformation.

- Stress Reduction: These techniques aren't just about anger; they're about reducing overall stress. As stress diminishes, so does the fuel that feeds your anger.

- Improved Mental Clarity: Mindfulness sharpens your mental focus and clarity, allowing you to respond to situations with thoughtfulness rather than react impulsively.

- Better Relationships: When you manage anger more effectively, your relationships with family, friends, and colleagues will benefit. You'll become a more understanding and empathetic presence in their lives.

As we journey together through this chapter, you'll encounter various mindfulness exercises, relaxation techniques, and guided practices that have the potential to transform your relationship with anger.

Just as that soft melody in the coffee shop guided me away from the brink of anger, the techniques you'll learn here can guide you toward a calmer, more centered existence.

So, are you ready to embark on this transformative journey into mindfulness and relaxation? Are you ready to discover the tools that can help you navigate the tempestuous sea of anger with newfound grace and serenity? Let's set sail and explore the peaceful shores of this invaluable chapter together.

Breathing Exercises

Imagine a moment of intense anger – a moment when your heart races, your muscles tense, and your thoughts become a tumultuous storm of frustration. In such moments, anger can feel overpowering, like a tempest threatening to consume you entirely. But what if I told you that one of the most potent tools for quelling this inner storm is as simple and accessible as your breath?

Be ready to delve into the remarkable world of breathing exercises – a cornerstone of mindfulness and relaxation techniques that can provide immediate relief during episodes of anger. These exercises are your lifeline when anger surges, helping you regain control and find a calm harbor within yourself.

The Power of Breath: Immediate Anger Diffusion

Before we explore specific breathing techniques, let's pause to understand the profound impact that our breath has on our emotional and physiological state. Have you ever noticed how your breathing changes when you're angry? It becomes shallow, rapid, and erratic.

This breathing pattern is closely linked to the "fight or flight" response triggered by anger.

When anger activates your "fight or flight" response, your body prepares to confront or escape a threat. Your heart rate increases, blood pressure rises, and muscles tense, all fueled by shallow, rapid breaths. While this response may be adaptive in genuine life-threatening situations, it can be counterproductive in everyday encounters that trigger anger.

Here's where conscious, deep breathing comes into play. By intentionally altering your breath pattern, you can send a powerful signal to your body that it's safe to relax. Deep, controlled breathing activates your body's parasympathetic nervous system, which is responsible for the "rest and digest" response. As a result, your heart rate decreases, blood pressure stabilizes, and muscles relax, creating a sense of calm and control.

Teaching Deep Breathing Techniques

Now, let's explore some deep breathing techniques that you can employ to diffuse anger in the heat of the moment. These techniques are easy to learn and can be practiced discreetly, allowing you to regain composure even in challenging situations.

The Four-Seven-Eight Breath:

1. Find a quiet space, if possible, or simply close your eyes for a moment.

2. Inhale through your nose quietly to a mental count of four.

3. Hold your breath for a count of seven.

4. Exhale completely through your mouth to a count of eight, making a soft whooshing sound.

5. Repeat this cycle three more times, or as needed.

The Four-Seven-Eight breath is a simple yet effective technique to soothe the nervous system and promote relaxation. It can be particularly helpful when you need a quick reset during a tense moment.

Box Breathing:

1. Imagine tracing a square with your breath, inhaling for a count of four, holding for four, exhaling for four, and pausing for four before inhaling again.

2. Visualize each side of the square as you follow the breath pattern.

Box breathing is a versatile technique that can be adapted to various situations. Its structured pattern helps anchor your focus and calm your mind.

Diaphragmatic Breathing:

1. Place one hand on your chest and the other on your abdomen.

2. Inhale deeply through your nose, allowing your abdomen to rise while keeping your chest still.

3. Exhale fully through your mouth, feeling your abdomen fall.

4. Continue this deep, rhythmic breathing for several breath cycles.

Diaphragmatic breathing is fundamental for cultivating awareness of your breath and calming your body's stress response.

Guided Breathing Exercises

To help you integrate these techniques, let's embark on a guided breathing exercise together. Find a comfortable seated position, close your eyes, and take a moment to ground yourself.

The Calming Wave Breath:

1. Imagine standing on a serene beach, with the gentle waves lapping at your feet.

2. Inhale deeply through your nose as you visualize the waves approaching the shore, filling your lungs with calmness.

3. Hold your breath for a moment, feeling the peace within you.

4. Exhale slowly through your mouth, watching the waves recede, releasing any tension or anger.

5. Continue this rhythmic breath, syncing with the ebb and flow of the imaginary waves.

This guided exercise taps into the soothing imagery of the ocean to help you find tranquility within. The act of syncing your breath with the visual can be a potent tool for immediate anger diffusion.

Incorporate these breathing exercises into your daily routine, practice them regularly, and make them your companions during moments of anger. The more you acquaint yourself with these techniques, the more readily available they will be when you need them most.

In the next section, we'll explore another relaxation technique to further enhance your journey towards mastering anger management: progressive muscle relaxation. This technique is particularly effective for releasing physical tension associated with anger and stress.

Progressive Muscle Relaxation

In the quest to master anger management, we've embarked on a journey into the realm of mindfulness and relaxation techniques. Thus far, we've explored the transformative power of deep breathing exercises, which provide immediate relief during moments of anger. Let's delve into another invaluable technique: Progressive Muscle Relaxation (PMR).

PMR is a simple yet highly effective practice that can help you release physical tension, calm your mind, and regain control over your emotional responses. As we journey, I'll guide you step by step through the process of PMR, elucidate its profound benefits in anger management, and even offer audio resources for your convenience.

Imagine carrying a heavy backpack filled with stones. With each step, the weight of the stones presses down on your shoulders, causing tension to accumulate. As the journey continues, your muscles become increasingly fatigued, and your body aches under the burden. This metaphor reflects how emotional baggage, stress, and anger can accumulate tension in our bodies over time.

Progressive Muscle Relaxation is like gradually unloading those heavy stones from your backpack. It's a systematic technique that involves tensing and then relaxing different muscle groups in your body. By doing so, you release stored physical tension, alleviate stress, and experience deep relaxation.

Step-by-Step Guide to Progressive Muscle Relaxation

Let's embark on a journey of relaxation by practicing Progressive Muscle Relaxation together. Find a quiet, comfortable space where you won't be disturbed. You can sit in a chair or lie on a flat surface, whichever feels most comfortable for you.

<u>Starting at the Toes</u>:

1. Close your eyes and take a few deep breaths to center yourself.

2. Begin by focusing on your toes. Curl them tightly, hold them for a few seconds, and then release them.

3. As you release, notice the sensation of relaxation spreading through your toes.

4. Continue to your feet, tightening the muscles, holding, and then releasing.

<u>Moving Up the Legs</u>:

1. Gradually work your way up, paying attention to each muscle group – the calves, thighs, and buttocks.

2. Tense each muscle group for about 5-7 seconds and then release, feeling the tension melt away.

<u>The Abdomen and Chest</u>:

1. Shift your focus to your abdominal muscles and tighten them, then release.

2. Move up to your chest, taking a deep breath and holding it for a moment before exhaling and letting go.

<u>The Arms and Hands</u>:

1. Progress to your arms, starting with your upper arms and forearms.

2. Make fists, squeeze your hands tightly, and then release.

3. Feel the tension draining from your fingertips.

<u>The Neck and Shoulders</u>:

1. Concentrate on your neck and shoulders, where many of us hold significant tension.

2. Shrug your shoulders up to your ears, hold, and then release, letting go of any accumulated stress.

The Face and Jaw:

1. Finally, turn your attention to your facial muscles. Scrunch up your face, squeeze your eyes shut, and clench your jaw.

2. Release and let your facial muscles go completely slack.

Full-Body Relaxation:

1. Take a few moments to scan your entire body, from your toes to the top of your head.

2. Notice how your body feels lighter, more relaxed, and free from tension.

As you complete this PMR exercise, you'll likely sense a profound shift in your physical and mental state. The burdens you carried – the metaphorical stones in your backpack – will have lightened considerably.

The Benefits of Tension Release in Anger Management

Progressive Muscle Relaxation offers several significant benefits when it comes to managing anger:

Physical Tension Reduction: PMR helps release the physical tension that often accompanies anger. This promotes relaxation and prevents the escalation of anger-related physical symptoms like headaches and muscle aches.

Stress Alleviation: By systematically relaxing your muscles, PMR triggers a relaxation response in your body. This reduces the production of stress hormones and fosters a sense of calm, making it easier to respond to anger triggers with composure.

Enhanced Self-Awareness: As you practice PMR regularly, you'll become more attuned to your body's physical sensations of tension and relaxation. This heightened awareness allows you to identify and address tension before it escalates into anger.

Improved Emotional Regulation: When you release physical tension through PMR, you'll find it easier to regulate your emotions. This can be especially valuable when dealing with anger-inducing situations.

Audio Resources for Guided Relaxation

To facilitate your practice of Progressive Muscle Relaxation, I've prepared audio resources that you can access and use at your convenience. These guided sessions will walk you through the PMR process, making it even more accessible and effective.

By incorporating PMR into your daily routine, you'll develop a valuable tool for managing anger, reducing stress, and achieving a greater sense of physical and emotional well-being. In the next section, we'll explore another aspect of relaxation – the power of visualization techniques in achieving calmness and serenity.

Visualization Techniques

As we continue our exploration of mindfulness and relaxation techniques, we arrive at the enchanting realm of Visualization Techniques. These practices harness the power of mental imagery to create a haven of serenity within. I'll illuminate the remarkable potential of visualization, guide you through crafting your personal calming visualizations, and share inspiring examples that have proven effective for many on their journey toward anger management.

The Magic of Mental Imagery

Have you ever closed your eyes and imagined yourself in a peaceful, idyllic setting? Perhaps you visualized a tranquil forest, the gentle sway of a hammock by the sea, or the warmth of a crackling fireplace. If so, you've already glimpsed the magic of mental imagery. Visualization techniques allow you to conjure vivid, multisensory images within your mind, creating a profound sense of relaxation and calm.

The power of visualization lies in its ability to engage your senses and emotions, tricking your mind into believing that you are genuinely experiencing the scenario you're picturing. As you immerse yourself in these calming visualizations, your body responds by releasing stress, reducing tension, and promoting a state of profound relaxation.

Creating Your Personal Calming Visualizations

Now, let's embark on a journey of crafting your personal calming visualizations. These mental landscapes will become your sanctuary – a place you can escape when anger or stress looms. Here's how to get started:

Step 1: <u>Choose Your Sanctuary</u>

Begin by selecting a calming and safe place that resonates with you. It could be a location from your past, a fictional setting from a favorite book or movie, or an entirely imaginary place. The key is that it should evoke feelings of tranquility and serenity within you.

Step 2: <u>Engage Your Senses</u>

Once you've chosen your sanctuary, it's time to fill it with sensory details. Close your eyes and imagine the sights, sounds, smells, textures, and even tastes that define this place. The more vivid and immersive your sensory experience, your visualization will be more effective.

Step 3: <u>Explore Mindfully</u>

Now, take a leisurely mental stroll through your sanctuary. Pay close attention to the details as you explore. Notice the play of light and shadow, the rustle of leaves, the scent of the air, and the warmth of the sun or the coziness of the space. Engage all your senses fully.

Step 4: Create a Mental Snapshot

Imagine capturing a mental snapshot of your sanctuary – a moment frozen in time. This could be a particularly serene scene, a place where you feel utterly safe, or an image that encapsulates the essence of your calming haven.

Step 5: Practice Regularly

Dedicate time each day to immerse yourself in your calming visualization. The more you practice, the more effortlessly you'll be able to slip into this mental sanctuary, even amid challenging situations.

Effective Visualization Scenarios

To offer inspiration and guidance, here are a few examples of effective visualization scenarios:

The Forest Retreat:

1. Picture yourself in a lush, tranquil forest. Tall trees provide shade, and the dappled sunlight dances on the forest floor.

2. You can hear the gentle rustle of leaves in the breeze and the distant song of a babbling brook.

3. The earthy scent of moss and fallen leaves fills the air, and the ground is soft beneath your feet.

4. As you wander deeper into the forest, you come across a tranquil clearing with a cozy blanket and a good book waiting for you.

The Beachside Oasis:

1. Imagine standing on a pristine, deserted beach at sunset. The waves lap at your feet, leaving a cool, refreshing sensation.

2. The sky is painted in orange, pink, and gold hues as the sun dips below the horizon.

3. Seagulls glide overhead, their calls blending harmoniously with the gentle crash of the waves.

4. A hammock sways invitingly between two palm trees, offering the perfect spot for relaxation.

<u>The Mountain Serenity</u>:

1. Envision yourself high in the mountains, surrounded by towering peaks and a clear, cerulean sky.

2. The air is crisp and invigorating as you hike along a peaceful trail.

3. You come across a serene alpine lake, its surface reflecting the surrounding peaks.

4. As you sit by the lake, you feel a profound sense of peace and connection with nature.

These visualization scenarios serve as starting points but feel free to create your personalized havens of tranquility. Your sanctuary should resonate deeply with your unique preferences and desires for relaxation.

As you practice visualization regularly, you'll discover its ability to transport you to a place of serenity, even when anger threatens to engulf you. In the next section, we'll explore another mindfulness practice – meditation – and its role in anger management.

Meditation for Anger Management

In the bustling cacophony of modern life, finding moments of stillness can feel like an elusive dream. Yet, it is in the serenity of these quiet moments that we often discover the greatest power – the power to manage our anger, harness our emotions, and cultivate a profound sense of inner calm. Welcome to the world of Meditation for Anger Management, where we will explore the transformative practice of meditation and how it can serve as your anchor amidst life's storms.

Before we delve into the heart of anger management meditation, we must acquaint ourselves with this ancient practice and its remarkable potential. Meditation is a versatile and accessible tool that individuals from all walks of life can embrace. It serves as a sanctuary for the mind, offering respite from daily existence's ceaseless chatter and chaos.

Suitable Techniques for Beginners

For those new to meditation, the prospect of quieting the mind may seem daunting. However, rest assured that meditation is a gentle and forgiving practice that welcomes beginners with open arms. Here are a few meditation techniques suitable for those taking their initial steps on this transformative journey:

<u>Mindfulness Meditation</u>: This foundational practice encourages you to focus on the present moment, observing thoughts and emotions without judgment. Mindfulness meditation is an excellent starting point for enhancing self-awareness and emotional regulation.

Guided Meditations: Guided meditations are led by experienced instructors who provide step-by-step instructions and soothing imagery to help you relax. These sessions are perfect for individuals who prefer structured guidance during their meditation practice.

Breath Awareness Meditation: As introduced earlier in our exploration of relaxation techniques, breath awareness meditation centers on the simple act of observing and controlling your breath. It's an effective method for grounding oneself in the present moment and reducing stress.

Loving-Kindness Meditation: Also known as Metta meditation, this practice focuses on cultivating feelings of love and compassion towards oneself and others. It's a powerful tool for transforming anger into understanding and empathy.

The Long-Term Benefits of Meditation

The profound impact of meditation on anger management extends far beyond immediate calming effects. Regular meditation practice can lead to a multitude of long-term benefits for both your emotional well-being and overall health:

Emotional Resilience: Meditation enhances your ability to navigate challenging emotions, such as anger, with grace and composure. It equips you with the tools to respond thoughtfully rather than react impulsively.

Stress Reduction: Chronic stress is often a breeding ground for anger. Meditation is a potent antidote to stress, as it activates the body's relaxation response, reducing the physiological triggers of anger.

Improved Emotional Regulation: You'll develop greater self-awareness and emotional intelligence through meditation. This heightened awareness allows you to recognize anger as it arises and respond skillfully.

Enhanced Focus and Concentration: Regular meditation sharpens your mental faculties, increasing your ability to maintain focus and remain calm in high-pressure situations.

Increased Empathy and Compassion: Meditation fosters feelings of empathy and compassion towards yourself and others. This shift in perspective can transform the way you perceive and manage anger.

Guided Meditation Scripts and Resources

To assist you in embarking on your meditation journey, here are a few guided meditation scripts and resources you can explore:

Basic Mindfulness Meditation:

1. Find a quiet, comfortable space and sit or lie down.

2. Close your eyes and take a few deep breaths to center yourself.

3. Shift your attention to your breath, observing each inhale and exhale without judgment.

4. If your mind wanders, gently guide your focus back to your breath.

5. Continue this practice for 10-15 minutes, gradually increasing the duration as you become more comfortable.

Loving-Kindness Meditation:

1. Sit in a comfortable position and close your eyes.

2. Begin by directing loving-kindness towards yourself. Silently repeat phrases like, "May I be happy, may I be healthy, may I live with ease."

3. Extend these well-wishes to loved ones, acquaintances, and even individuals you may have conflicts with.

4. Allow your heart to be open to the possibility of compassion for all beings.

Meditation Apps and Online Resources:

A wealth of meditation apps and online platforms offer guided meditations suitable for beginners. Explore options like Headspace, Calm, Insight Timer, and many more. As you embark on your meditation journey, remember that consistency and patience are your allies. Just as a river gradually shapes the landscape over time, meditation gradually transforms your inner landscape.

Cultivating Mindfulness

Picture this: You're driving home from work, stuck in traffic, and the minutes seem to stretch endlessly. Your frustration builds with each passing moment, and your temper flares. Sound familiar? It's a scenario we've all experienced at some point, a minor inconvenience that can send us spiraling into anger. But what if there was a way to navigate these situations gracefully, to transform anger into patience and understanding? This is where the power of mindfulness enters the stage.

Understanding Mindfulness and Its Relevance to Anger

Mindfulness is not a buzzword or a passing trend; it's a profound practice rooted in ancient traditions and supported by modern science. At its core, mindfulness is the art of being fully present in the moment with an open heart and non-judgmental awareness. It involves observing your thoughts, feelings, and sensations as they arise without trying to suppress or amplify them.

In the context of anger management, mindfulness is a game-changer. Here's why:

1. <u>Recognizing Anger Triggers</u>: Mindfulness heightens your awareness of internal and external triggers. It allows you to identify the precise moment anger begins to stir, long before it erupts into full-blown fury. This heightened awareness enables you to intercept and manage anger more effectively.

2. <u>Emotional Regulation</u>: You develop emotional regulation skills by practicing mindfulness. Instead of reacting impulsively to anger, you learn to respond thoughtfully and calmly. This shift in your emotional response can defuse even the most volatile situations.

3. <u>Reducing Impulsive Reactions</u>: Mindfulness promotes a pause between stimulus and response. In this pause, you can choose your reaction consciously rather than succumbing to automatic and potentially regrettable responses.

Practical Exercises for Incorporating Mindfulness into Daily Life

Mindfulness isn't limited to sitting meditation; it's a way of life. Here are practical exercises to help you integrate mindfulness into your daily routine:

1. <u>Mindful Breathing</u>: This exercise can be practiced anywhere, anytime. Pause for a few moments and focus your attention on your breath. Feel the sensation of each inhale and exhale. If your mind wanders, gently bring it back to your breath. This practice can help ground you in moments of anger.

2. <u>Body Scan</u>: Dedicate a few minutes daily to a body scan. Start at the top of your head and slowly move your attention down through your body, noticing any tension or discomfort. This practice fosters awareness of physical sensations, which can be closely linked to anger.

3. <u>Mindful Eating</u>: During your next meal, eat slowly and deliberately. Pay attention to the flavors, textures, and sensations of each bite. Mindful eating enhances your connection with food and encourages you to savor the present moment.

4. <u>Daily Mindful Check-Ins</u>: Set aside a few moments in the morning and evening to check in with yourself. Ask how you're feeling emotionally and physically. This practice fosters self-awareness and helps you recognize patterns of anger triggers.

Stories of Transformation Through Mindfulness

The journey to anger management through mindfulness has transformed countless lives. Let's explore some real-life stories of individuals who embraced mindfulness and rewrote their relationship with anger:

Sarah's Story: Sarah had a high-stress job that often left her seething with anger. A friend introduced her to mindfulness, and she began meditating daily. Over time, Sarah noticed she could navigate work challenges more calmly and clearly. Mindfulness allowed her to retreat from heated moments and respond to conflicts gracefully and compassion.

David's Transformation: David had a short fuse and frequently clashed with his teenage son. He learned to pause and listen attentively through mindfulness when his son expressed himself. This simple act of mindful listening opened channels of communication they had never experienced before, bringing them closer and diffusing anger-driven arguments.

Maria's Journey: Maria's life was marked by chronic anger stemming from unresolved childhood trauma. Mindfulness therapy enabled her to explore these deep-seated emotions with gentleness and acceptance. Through her mindfulness practice, she gradually released the grip of anger and found healing and peace.

As you embark on your mindfulness journey, remember that it's not about achieving perfection; it's about progress. Start small, be patient with yourself, and allow mindfulness to infuse your life with a sense of presence and awareness.

Chapter Five
COGNITIVE BEHAVIORAL TECHNIQUES

Close your eyes for a moment and imagine this: You're in the middle of a heated argument with someone you care about. Your heart races, your jaw clenches, and your frustration surges like a tidal wave. It feels as though anger has taken the reins, leaving you powerless in its grip. Sound familiar?

Welcome to the world of Cognitive Behavioral Techniques (CBT), a chapter in your journey toward mastering anger management. As you'll soon discover, CBT offers a powerful toolkit for understanding and transforming your relationship with anger.

Before we delve into the science and strategies behind CBT, let me share a personal story that explains why I've dedicated a chapter of this book to CBT.

Not too long ago, I was caught in a cycle of anger that I couldn't escape. Small annoyances snowballed into rage, and I often lashed out at the people I loved most. I knew I needed a change, but the path forward was unclear.

One day, while searching for answers, I stumbled upon the world of Cognitive Behavioral Techniques. It promised a way out of the anger labyrinth, a way to rewire my habitual responses and regain control over my emotions.

I started applying CBT principles to my life, and slowly but surely, I noticed a transformation. The power that anger held over me began to wane. I learned to challenge my thought patterns, identify triggers, and choose more constructive responses. My relationships improved, and I felt a newfound sense of inner peace.

This personal journey led me to write this chapter and share the life-changing insights and techniques that helped me conquer my anger. I want you to experience the same sense of liberation and empowerment CBT has brought me.

In the pages ahead, we'll dive deep into the world of Cognitive Behavioral Techniques, offering you a comprehensive understanding of:

- Identifying Cognitive Distortions: We'll explore common cognitive distortions that fuel anger and provide practical exercises for recognizing and challenging these distortions. Understanding the thought patterns behind your anger will give you valuable insights into your emotional reactions.

- The ABC Model (Antecedent, Belief, Consequence): We'll introduce you to the ABC model of cognitive behavioral therapy, a powerful tool for dissecting and understanding the events that trigger your anger. Through real-life examples, you'll learn how to apply this model to your anger-inducing situations.

- Thought Records: You'll discover the transformative potential of thought records. We'll guide you through the process of keeping thought records to track anger patterns, identify triggers, and reshape your cognitive responses. Thought records are a practical and effective way to break free from destructive thought patterns.

- Problem-Solving Strategies: Anger often stems from unresolved issues and frustrations. In this chapter, we'll provide a step-by-step approach to problem-solving, helping you address the root causes of your anger and prevent escalation.

- Assertiveness Training: We'll distinguish between assertiveness and aggression, offering scripts and role-playing exercises for assertive communication. By mastering assertiveness, you'll navigate conflicts with confidence and diplomacy.

As you read through these techniques, you'll gain a comprehensive understanding of CBT and practical tools to implement in your daily life. The benefits are profound: improved relationships, reduced stress, enhanced emotional regulation, and a newfound sense of control over your anger responses.

So, are you ready to embark on this journey of self-discovery and transformation? The tools you need to rewire your anger response are within your reach, and they await you in the pages of this chapter. Let's explore the world of Cognitive Behavioral Techniques together and unlock the doors to a calmer, more empowered you.

Identifying Cognitive Distortions

Imagine You're stuck in a traffic jam, running late for an important meeting. Frustration mounts, your heart races, and a boiling sensation creep up your neck. You might find yourself thinking, "This is a disaster! Everything is ruined!"

What you've just experienced is a classic example of cognitive distortions at work, and they play a significant role in fueling anger. We'll embark on a journey to uncover these hidden culprits, understand how they contribute to anger, and, most importantly, learn how to challenge and reframe them.

Cognitive distortions are automatic and often irrational thought patterns that influence our perceptions of events and situations. They can distort reality, leading us to jump to negative conclusions, catastrophize, or perceive threats where none exist. These distorted thoughts contribute significantly to our experience of anger.

Common Cognitive Distortions That Fuel Anger

All-or-Nothing Thinking (Black-and-White Thinking): This distortion involves viewing situations in extreme, either-or terms, with no middle ground. For example, believing that making a small mistake means you're a total failure.

Catastrophizing (Magnification and Minimization): Catastrophizing involves blowing things out of proportion or minimizing their importance. For instance, you might see a minor setback as an absolute disaster.

Overgeneralization: Overgeneralization involves drawing sweeping conclusions based on a single negative event. For instance, if someone rejects your invitation, you may conclude that no one ever wants to spend time with you.

Mental Filtering (Selective Abstraction): This distortion focuses exclusively on negative aspects of a situation while ignoring any positive elements. For example, you might receive a positive performance review but dwell only on a single critical comment.

Discounting the Positive: This distortion entails dismissing positive experiences, achievements, or feedback as irrelevant or insignificant. You might reject compliments or undermine your accomplishments by saying, "It was just luck."

Mind Reading: Mind reading involves assuming you know what others are thinking or feeling without concrete evidence. For instance, believing that your friend is angry with you because they haven't returned your message.

Emotional Reasoning: Emotional reasoning occurs when you believe that your feelings accurately reflect reality, regardless of evidence to the contrary. For example, if you feel like a failure, you conclude that you must be one.

Should Statements: This distortion involves imposing rigid, unrealistic expectations on yourself or others. When you use phrases like "I should," "I must," or "They should," you create undue pressure and set yourself up for disappointment.

Labeling and Mislabeling: Labeling and mislabeling involve attaching negative labels to yourself or others based on past behavior or mistakes. Instead of acknowledging that you made a mistake, you might label yourself as "a failure."

Personalization: Personalization involves attributing external events, especially negative ones, to yourself as if you are solely responsible. For instance, you might blame yourself for a colleague's bad mood.

Unmasking Cognitive Distortions with Worksheets

One powerful tool for identifying and challenging cognitive distortions is the use of worksheets. These structured exercises help you become more aware of your thought patterns and provide a framework for shifting them. Let's briefly explore a few of these worksheets:

Thought Record Worksheet: This tool prompts you to identify a distressing situation, record your automatic thoughts and emotions, analyze the cognitive distortions at play, and develop more balanced and rational responses.

Daily Mood Journal: A daily mood journal encourages you to track your emotions throughout the day and the events or thoughts that trigger them. Over time, this journal helps you recognize patterns and connections between your mood and cognitive distortions.

Challenging Beliefs Worksheet: This worksheet guides you in questioning the validity of your negative beliefs by asking probing questions, such as "Is there any evidence to support this thought?" or "What's the worst that could happen, and how likely is it?"

Real-Life Examples of Cognitive Restructuring

To illustrate the effectiveness of cognitive restructuring, let's delve into a couple of real-life scenarios where individuals identified and challenged their cognitive distortions:

Example 1: Overcoming Catastrophizing

Susan, a working professional, had a habit of catastrophizing work-related issues. She believed her entire career was in jeopardy whenever she made a mistake. Through cognitive restructuring, Susan learned to ask herself, "What's the worst that could happen?" She realized that even if she made an occasional mistake, it didn't diminish her overall competence. This shift in thinking reduced her anxiety and improved her job satisfaction.

Example 2: Dispelling All-or-Nothing Thinking

Mark, a student, often engaged in all-or-nothing thinking regarding academic performance. He saw it as a complete failure if he didn't get a perfect score on a test. With the help of cognitive restructuring exercises, Mark started acknowledging that perfection wasn't attainable and that making mistakes was a natural part of learning. This change in perspective reduced his fear of failure and allowed him to approach his studies with greater resilience.

By recognizing these cognitive distortions in their thought patterns, Susan and Mark could challenge and reframe their beliefs, leading to more rational and constructive responses. These real-life examples show the tangible benefits of cognitive restructuring in managing anger and improving overall emotional well-being.

As you continue your journey through this chapter, you'll gain a deeper understanding of these cognitive distortions, work through practical exercises, and learn how to apply cognitive restructuring techniques to transform your relationship with anger. Remember, by unmasking these hidden culprits, you take a significant step toward mastering your anger and finding greater peace within yourself.

The ABC Model (Antecedent, Belief, Consequence)

Imagine this scenario: You're stuck in a crowded, noisy, and slow-moving line at the grocery store. Your patience wears thin as you watch the minutes tick away. Frustration bubbles up, and you can feel anger building inside you. But why? What's causing this surge of emotion?

The ABC Model, a fundamental cognitive behavioral therapy (CBT) concept, offers insights into understanding the intricate interplay of our thoughts, emotions, and reactions, especially in anger-inducing situations. We'll delve into the ABC Model, dissecting its components and equipping you with the tools to apply it effectively in your daily life.

Unveiling the ABC Model

The ABC Model is a framework used in CBT to explore and make sense of our emotional responses. It breaks down the sequence of events leading to an emotional reaction into three key elements:

<u>Antecedent</u> (A): This represents the triggering event or situation that initiates the emotional response. The external or internal circumstance sets the stage for your emotions.

Belief (B): Beliefs are the thoughts, interpretations, or perceptions you attach to the triggering event. They can be rational or irrational and heavily influence your emotional reaction.

Consequence (C): Consequence refers to the emotional and behavioral outcome of your beliefs about the antecedent. This is where you experience anger, sadness, anxiety, or any other emotion, and it can lead to specific actions or reactions.

Decoding the Anger Equation with the ABC Model

Let's revisit the grocery store scenario through the lens of the ABC Model:

Antecedent (A): Waiting in the long, slow-moving grocery store line.

Belief (B): "This is unacceptable. It's wasting my time, and people are so inconsiderate. I can't stand this!"

Consequence (C): You become increasingly frustrated and angry, perhaps muttering complaints under your breath or clenching your fists.

Here, you can see how your beliefs (B) about the situation (A) led to your emotional consequence (C) of anger. The ABC Model helps you recognize that it's not the external event but your interpretation and beliefs that drive your emotional reactions.

Applying the ABC Model to Anger-Inducing Situations

To effectively manage anger using the ABC Model, follow these steps:

Step 1: Identify the Antecedent (A)

 1. Pay attention to what's happening around you when you

start to feel angry.

2. Note the specific circumstances, people, or events that trigger your anger.

Step 2: Examine Your Beliefs (B)

1. Reflect on the thoughts and interpretations you associate with the antecedent.

2. Ask yourself: What am I telling myself about this situation?

3. Challenge irrational or unhelpful beliefs by considering alternative, more balanced perspectives.

Step 3: Analyze the Consequence (C)

1. Explore the emotions and physical sensations you experience due to your beliefs.

2. Recognize the impact of your anger on your behavior and well-being.

Step 4: Reframe and Restructure (Practice the ABC Model)

1. Practice the ABC Model by consciously challenging and reframing your beliefs when you identify them as leading to anger.

2. Replace irrational beliefs with rational, balanced thoughts.

3. Consider the consequences of your beliefs and choose healthier emotional responses.

Exercises for Practicing the ABC Model

Anger Journal: Keep a journal to record instances when you feel angry. Describe the antecedent, your beliefs, and the consequences. Over time, look for patterns and practice reframing your beliefs.

Role-Playing: Enlist a trusted friend or therapist to role-play anger-inducing scenarios. Practice identifying the ABC components and explore alternative beliefs and reactions.

Mindfulness Meditation: Engage in mindfulness meditation to increase your awareness of the present moment. Mindfulness can help you observe your thoughts and emotions without judgment, making identifying and modifying your beliefs easier.

By regularly applying the ABC Model, you'll gain deeper insights into the sources of your anger and develop the skills needed to respond more constructively. It's a powerful tool that empowers you to take control of your emotional responses, transform irrational beliefs, and ultimately find greater peace within yourself. As we proceed through this chapter, we'll continue to explore practical techniques and exercises to strengthen your cognitive-behavioral skills in managing anger.

Thought Records

Imagine if you could unveil the intricate workings of your mind like a detective deciphering a complex case. Well, with the help of thought records, you can do just that. Thought records are invaluable tools in the realm of cognitive behavioral therapy (CBT), providing a structured approach to untangling your thoughts, emotions, and behaviors, especially when it comes to managing anger.

I'll show you the world of thought records, guiding you through their use, discussing their ability to unearth your anger triggers, and offering templates to get you started on your journey toward a calmer, more mindful you.

Unveiling the Power of Thought Records

Thought records, sometimes called thought diaries or thought logs, are systematically recording your thoughts, feelings, and behaviors in specific situations. The goal is to gain insight into the connections between your beliefs and emotional reactions. Doing so allows you to identify patterns, recognize triggers, and ultimately transform unhelpful thought patterns into healthier ones.

How to Keep a Thought Record

Identify the Situation: Describe the situation or event that triggered your anger. Be as specific as possible. What happened, where were you, who was involved, and what were you doing?

Identify Your Thoughts: Record the thoughts that went through your mind during the situation. Pay attention to self-talk, inner dialogue, or any automatic thoughts. What were you saying to yourself about the situation?

Emotions and Intensity: Note the emotions you experienced during the situation. Rate the intensity of each emotion on a scale from 0 to 100, with 0 being no intensity and 100 being extreme intensity.

Physical Sensations: Describe any physical sensations or bodily reactions you noticed. Did you experience tension, sweating, increased heart rate, or other physical symptoms?

Behaviors and Actions: Document your behaviors or actions in response to your thoughts and emotions. How did you behave outwardly? Did you react aggressively, passively, or assertively?

Alternative Thoughts: Challenge your initial thoughts by generating more balanced or rational alternatives. Ask yourself if there's a different way to interpret the situation.

Re-rate Emotions: After considering alternative thoughts, re-rate the intensity of your emotions. Did challenging your thoughts lead to a change in emotional intensity?

Unearthing Triggers and Responses

Let's explore how thought records can reveal your anger triggers and responses with an example:

Situation: You're driving home in heavy traffic, and someone cuts in front of you without using a turn signal.

Thoughts: "This guy is such an idiot! He's trying to ruin my day. He doesn't care about anyone else on the road."

Emotions and Intensity: Anger (90), frustration (85), irritation (80).

Physical Sensations: Increased heart rate, clenched fists, shallow breathing.

Behaviors and Actions: Honking the horn, tailgating the driver, yelling profanities.

Alternative Thoughts: "Maybe he didn't see me, or he's in a rush for an emergency. Getting angry won't change anything. I'll just focus on my driving."

Re-rate Emotions: Anger (60), frustration (55), irritation (50).

In this example, the initial thoughts and emotional intensity were overwhelmingly negative and intense. However, the emotional intensity decreased significantly by challenging these thoughts with more balanced alternatives. The thought record helped uncover the trigger (reckless driving) and the response (anger), allowing for a more constructive and controlled reaction.

Templates for Thought Records

Below are templates you can use for thought records:

Situation: Describe the triggering event or situation.

Thoughts: Record the thoughts that went through your mind.

Emotions and Intensity: List the emotions and rate their intensity.

Physical Sensations: Document any physical sensations or bodily reactions.

Behaviors and Actions: Describe your outward behaviors or actions.

Alternative Thoughts: Challenge your initial thoughts with more balanced alternatives.

Re-rate Emotions: After considering alternative thoughts, re-rate the emotional intensity.

You'll gain valuable insights into your anger patterns by consistently using thought records. Over time, you'll become more skilled at recognizing and modifying unhelpful thought patterns, leading to more constructive emotional responses.

Problem-Solving Strategies

Imagine this scenario: You're stuck in traffic, running late for an important meeting, and your frustration is mounting with each passing minute. As anger starts to boil within, you may find yourself gripping the steering wheel tighter, cursing at the cars around you, or even laying on the horn. It's a classic situation where anger can escalate rapidly. But what if there was a better way to handle it? Enter problem-solving strategies—a powerful tool for defusing anger and resolving life's challenges.

We will embark on a journey through problem-solving techniques that can prevent anger escalation, improve decision-making, and enhance your overall anger management skills. By the end, you'll have a clear roadmap to tackle life's obstacles with a composed mind.

Problem-solving is the process of finding effective solutions to the difficulties and challenges you encounter in life. It's a structured and systematic approach that helps you overcome obstacles and minimizes the emotional turmoil that can accompany unresolved problems. When applied effectively, problem-solving can be your best friend in managing anger.

Step-by-Step Approach to Problem-Solving

Problem-solving is often simplified into a series of steps. While these steps may vary slightly depending on the source, the core elements remain consistent:

<u>Identify the Problem</u>: The first and most crucial step is recognizing and clearly defining the problem. Understanding what you're dealing with is essential before attempting to solve it.

<u>Generate Possible Solutions</u>: Brainstorm various potential solutions or courses of action. Be creative and consider multiple options, no matter how unconventional they may seem.

<u>Evaluate the Solutions</u>: Examine each potential solution critically. Assess their advantages, disadvantages, and potential consequences. Look for potential roadblocks or unintended outcomes.

<u>Select the Best Solution</u>: Based on your evaluation, choose the most viable and appropriate solution for the situation. Trust your judgment and instincts.

<u>Create an Action Plan</u>: Develop a detailed plan for implementing your chosen solution. Outline the specific steps you need to take, the resources required, and a timeline.

<u>Implement the Solution</u>: Put your action plan into motion. Take the necessary steps to address the problem, and stay focused on your chosen solution.

<u>Evaluate the Outcome</u>: After implementing the solution, assess the results. Did it work as expected? If not, what adjustments or alternative solutions are needed?

<u>Learn and Adapt</u>: Use the experience as an opportunity for growth. Learn from the process and adjust your problem-solving skills for future challenges.

Problem-Solving and Anger Escalation

So, how does problem-solving relate to anger management? The connection lies in the fact that unresolved problems and unmet needs can fuel anger. When you're faced with a frustrating situation or obstacle, anger may arise as a natural response. However, by employing effective problem-solving techniques, you can address the root causes of your anger and prevent it from escalating.

Practical Application and Exercises

Let's put problem-solving into practice with a real-life scenario:

Problem: You frequently find yourself overwhelmed with work, leading to stress and irritability.

Step 1 - Identify the Problem: Recognize that your workload is causing stress and impacting your mood.

Step 2 - Generate Possible Solutions: Brainstorm options, such as delegating tasks, prioritizing projects, or discussing your workload with a supervisor.

Step 3 - Evaluate the Solutions: Consider the pros and cons of each solution. Delegating tasks may reduce your workload but could require training others. Prioritizing projects might help manage your time better but could still leave you with a heavy workload.

Step 4 - Select the Best Solution: Based on your evaluation, you decide to discuss your workload with your supervisor to explore options for lightening your responsibilities.

Step 5 - Create an Action Plan: Schedule a meeting with your supervisor to discuss your concerns and potential solutions. Prepare talking points and propose a plan for redistributing tasks.

Step 6 - Implement the Solution: During the meeting, communicate your concerns and propose solutions. Collaborate with your supervisor to develop a plan for managing your workload.

Step 7 - Evaluate the Outcome: After implementing the plan, assess whether your workload has decreased and your stress levels have improved.

Step 8 - Learn and Adapt: Reflect on the experience and consider what worked and what didn't. Use this knowledge to refine your problem-solving skills for future challenges.

By applying this problem-solving approach to various aspects of your life, you'll address issues that trigger anger and cultivate a proactive and adaptive mindset. This mindset will be a powerful ally in effectively managing anger and preventing its escalation.

Assertiveness Training

Imagine this scenario: You're at a family gathering, and a relative starts making unwelcome remarks about your choices in life. Your initial reaction might be to seethe in silence, respond with passive-aggressiveness, or explode in anger. However, there's a more constructive way to handle such situations—assertiveness. We'll explore assertiveness training, a vital skill in managing anger effectively.

Distinguishing Between Assertiveness and Aggression

Before delving into assertiveness training, it's crucial to understand the fundamental difference between assertiveness and aggression. These two communication styles are often confused, but they yield vastly different results:

Aggression: Aggressive communication involves expressing your needs, wants, or opinions forcefully, often at the expense of others. It may include yelling, blaming, or using hurtful language. Aggression seeks to dominate or intimidate, rarely producing positive outcomes.

Assertiveness: On the other hand, assertive communication is about expressing your thoughts, feelings, and needs honestly and respectfully while respecting the rights and boundaries of others. It promotes open and constructive dialogue and aims for mutual understanding and compromise.

The Power of Assertive Communication

Assertiveness is a skill that can be honed and used in various aspects of life, from personal relationships to the workplace. When you communicate assertively, you:

Express Yourself Clearly: You convey your thoughts, feelings, and needs with clarity, ensuring that your message is understood.

Respect Boundaries: You recognize and respect the boundaries of others while maintaining your own. This fosters healthy, balanced interactions.

Build Self-Esteem: Assertiveness allows you to stand up for yourself respectfully, boosting your self-esteem and self-worth.

Resolve Conflicts: Assertive communication is an effective tool for resolving conflicts and reaching mutually beneficial solutions.

Scripts and Role-Playing Exercises for Assertive Communication

Becoming assertive requires practice and guidance. To help you develop this skill, we'll provide scripts and role-playing exercises that you can use in various situations.

Scenario 1: Expressing Disagreement

Imagine you're in a meeting at work, and a colleague suggests an idea that you believe will not work. Instead of staying silent or immediately shooting down their idea, consider the following assertive response:

Script: "I appreciate your suggestion, and I can see how it might be beneficial. However, I have some concerns about its feasibility, and I'd like to discuss them with you. Can we take some time to explore other options together?"

Scenario 2: Setting Personal Boundaries

In personal relationships, it's essential to establish and maintain boundaries. If a friend frequently calls you late at night, interrupting your sleep, and you want to address this issue assertively, try this script:

Script: "I value our friendship, and I enjoy our conversations. However, I need to set a boundary regarding late-night calls, as it affects my sleep. I'd appreciate it if we could schedule our chats during more suitable times. I hope you understand."

Scenario 3: Dealing with Criticism

Responding to criticism can be challenging, but assertive communication can help maintain your self-respect. If someone criticizes your choices or actions, consider this script:

Script: "I understand that you have concerns about my decision, and I value your perspective. However, I believe this choice is right for me, and I've considered the consequences. I'd appreciate your support and understanding, even if you disagree."

Real-Life Stories of Assertiveness in Action

To illustrate the power of assertiveness, here are a couple of real-life stories where individuals used assertive communication to diffuse potential anger situations:

Story 1: Navigating a Challenging Conversation

Sarah found herself in a heated discussion with a coworker who repeatedly interrupted her during meetings. Sarah decided to use assertive communication instead of reacting with frustration or anger. She said, "I value our discussions, but I've noticed that I'm often interrupted. I need to express my thoughts without interruptions to ensure we have productive conversations. Can we work together to maintain a respectful dialogue?"

The coworker appreciated Sarah's approach, and their meetings became more constructive due to this assertive interaction.

Story 2: Setting Boundaries in a Friendship

John had a close friend who frequently borrowed money without paying it back. Instead of harboring resentment, John chose to have an assertive conversation. He said, "I care about our friendship, but I've noticed that loans between us often go unpaid, which makes me uncomfortable. I need to set a boundary and refrain from lending money. I hope you understand that this decision is about preserving our friendship."

By addressing the issue assertively, John maintained the friendship while also protecting his boundaries.

These real-life examples demonstrate that assertiveness can defuse potential anger and lead to more positive outcomes in various situations. It's a valuable skill that empowers you to communicate effectively while preserving your self-respect and the integrity of your relationships.

Chapter Six
Emotional Intelligence and Anger

Amidst the chaos of modern life, with its relentless demands and unexpected challenges, I found myself grappling with a powerful adversary—my anger. It was a force that threatened to engulf me, causing turmoil in my personal and professional life. I knew I had to find a way to tame this tempestuous emotion, and my journey led me to a profound realization—emotional intelligence was the key to navigating the storm within.

Picture a rainy day when I was stuck in traffic, late for an important meeting. My heart pounded, and my hands clenched the steering wheel as impatience and frustration coursed through me. My thoughts spiraled into a maelstrom of negativity, and I honked my horn in futile rage.

At that moment, anger was in the driver's seat, and I was a mere passenger on a turbulent journey. It was a wake-up call that forced me to confront a pressing question: How could I gain mastery over my emotions and prevent them from hijacking my life?

Chapter 5 delves deep into the fascinating realm of emotional intelligence and its pivotal role in managing anger effectively. It explores how understanding and harnessing our emotions can lead to more harmonious relationships, improved well-being, and personal growth.

Emotional intelligence isn't just a buzzword; it's a life skill that can transform how you navigate the world. In this chapter, we will embark on a journey to:

- Understand Emotions: We'll unravel the complex tapestry of human emotions, including anger, exploring their origins and significance.

- Develop Self-Awareness: You'll discover how to recognize and understand your own emotions, a critical first step in managing them effectively.

- Enhance Empathy: We'll explore the art of empathy, enabling you to connect more deeply with others and build stronger relationships.

- Regulate Emotions: You'll gain practical strategies for managing and controlling your emotions, especially anger, in various situations.

- Cultivate Social Skills: We'll discuss the importance of effective communication, conflict resolution, and assertiveness in fostering healthier interactions.

By the time you finish this chapter, you will have the tools and insights needed to enhance your emotional intelligence and gain mastery over your anger. You'll be better equipped to:

- Identify Triggers: Recognize the emotional triggers that lead to anger and respond to them with greater self-awareness.

- Navigate Conflict: Approach conflicts calmly and empathetically, diffusing tension and promoting understanding.

- Foster Healthy Relationships: Build stronger, more meaningful relationships by connecting on an emotional level and communicating effectively.

- Promote Personal Growth: Use emotional intelligence as a catalyst for personal growth, helping you become the best version of yourself.

As we explore the fascinating world of emotional intelligence and its profound impact on anger management, I'll share stories illustrating its practical application. These stories will provide real-life examples of individuals who transformed their lives by embracing emotional intelligence.

So, fasten your seatbelts, for we are about to embark on a transformative journey into the depths of emotional intelligence. This journey will empower you to navigate the storm within and emerge stronger, wiser, and more in control of your emotions.

Understanding Emotions

In the vast landscape of human experience, emotions reign supreme. They color our world, drive our actions, and shape our interactions with others. Emotions are the very essence of what makes us human. Yet, understanding them and harnessing their power can be a complex and transformative journey that lies at emotional intelligence's heart.

The Spectrum of Emotion

Emotions are not singular entities but a spectrum of nuanced experiences. They range from the exuberance of joy to the depths of despair, from the fiery intensity of anger to the soothing calm of contentment. To navigate this complex terrain effectively, we must first grasp the concept of emotional intelligence.

Emotional intelligence, often abbreviated as EQ (Emotional Quotient), is the capacity to recognize, understand, manage, and utilize our own emotions and those of others in constructive ways. It involves being in touch with your feelings and having the ability to interpret and respond to the emotions of those around you. At its core, emotional intelligence is about enhancing self-awareness and interpersonal relationships.

Exercises for Emotional Awareness

Developing emotional intelligence begins with honing our emotional awareness. The more attuned we are to our feelings and those of others, the better equipped we become to manage them effectively. Here are a few exercises to kickstart your journey to heightened emotional awareness:

Emotion Journal: Start by maintaining a journal where you jot down your daily emotional experiences. What triggered your emotions?

How did you react? Over time, patterns may emerge that shed light on recurring emotional responses.

Mindful Meditation: Dedicate a few minutes each day to mindfulness meditation. This practice encourages you to focus on the present moment and become more in tune with your emotions as they arise. It also promotes emotional regulation.

Emotion Charades: Engage in an "emotion charades" game with friends or family. Take turns acting out various emotions without using words, and have others guess what you're expressing. This playful exercise enhances your emotional expression and recognition skills.

Empathy: The Bridge to Understanding

Empathy, often regarded as the cornerstone of emotional intelligence, is the ability to recognize and share the feelings of others. The bridge connects us to the emotions of those around us, fostering deeper connections and more effective communication. When it comes to managing anger, empathy plays a crucial role.

The Role of Empathy in Managing Anger

Imagine a situation where someone close to you is expressing frustration or anger. Without empathy, your response might be defensive or dismissive, escalating the conflict further. However, when you approach the situation with empathy, you can understand that their anger stems from their own emotional experience.

Empathy allows you to:

<u>Listen Actively</u>: Instead of reacting defensively, you actively listen to the other person's perspective. You strive to understand the emotions driving their words and actions.

<u>Validate Emotions</u>: Empathy enables you to acknowledge the validity of the other person's feelings, even if you don't necessarily agree with their point of view.

<u>De-escalate Tension</u>: You create a space for open and honest communication by showing empathy. This often leads to the de-escalation of anger and a more constructive dialogue.

Exercising Empathy

Enhancing your empathy is a vital aspect of managing anger effectively. Here are some exercises to help you develop and strengthen your empathetic skills:

<u>The Empathy Challenge</u>: Challenge yourself to put yourself in someone else's shoes regularly. When you encounter a situation that elicits an emotional response in another person, pause and try to understand their perspective and feelings.

<u>Reflective Listening</u>: Practice reflective listening in your conversations. When someone shares their thoughts and emotions, reflect back on what you've heard to confirm your understanding and show that you are actively engaged in their experience.

<u>Empathy Journal</u>: Keep an empathy journal to record instances when you successfully empathized with others. Note the outcomes of these empathetic interactions and how they contributed to better understanding and reduced conflict.

Empathy Stories: Real-Life Transformations

Throughout this chapter, we'll explore real-life stories of individuals who have harnessed the power of emotional intelligence and empathy to transform their lives and manage anger effectively. These stories are inspirational examples of how empathy can diffuse anger, heal relationships, and foster personal growth.

As we delve deeper into emotional intelligence and empathy, you'll discover that these skills are essential for managing anger and creating a more harmonious and fulfilling life. The journey to understanding emotions and embracing empathy is a profound one that promises personal growth, enriched relationships, and a deeper connection to the world around you.

Managing Emotional Responses

Emotions, the ever-present currents in the river of life, often carry us away without warning. These surges of intense emotion can be particularly challenging to navigate when it comes to anger. However, within the realm of emotional intelligence lies the powerful skill of managing emotional responses effectively. Let's explore techniques and strategies that will not only help you manage strong emotional responses, particularly anger but also prevent the all-too-common emotional hijackings that can disrupt our lives.

The Challenge of Emotional Responses

Emotional responses are an integral part of being human. They can be gentle and comforting, like the sun's soothing warmth on a spring day, or stormy and turbulent, like a thunderstorm raging through the night. Anger, in particular, has the potential to be one of the most destructive emotional storms we encounter.

Preventing Emotional Hijacking

Emotional hijacking occurs when our emotions overwhelm our rational thinking, leading to impulsive and often regrettable reactions. It's like being caught in a sudden downpour without an umbrella. To prevent emotional hijacking, it's essential to cultivate emotional self-regulation, the ability to control our emotions instead of letting them control us.

Techniques for Managing Strong Emotional Responses

Emotion Awareness: The first step in managing strong emotional responses is to become acutely aware of your emotions as they arise. This heightened awareness allows you to recognize the initial signs of emotional arousal, such as a racing heart, shallow breathing, or muscle tension.

Mindful Breathing: When you feel a surge of anger or other intense emotions, pause and focus on your breath. Take slow, deep breaths to calm the physiological responses triggered by the emotion. Deep breathing has a remarkable impact on calming the storm within.

Choice and Response: One hallmark of emotional intelligence is recognizing that you have a choice in how you respond to your emotions. You can either react impulsively, allowing the emotion to dictate your actions, or you can choose to respond thoughtfully and intentionally.

Distract and Detach: Sometimes, stepping away from the emotionally charged situation provides the necessary emotional distance to regain composure. This can be as simple as excusing yourself for a few moments to collect your thoughts.

Empathy and Evaluation: Try to empathize with the perspective of others involved in the situation. Evaluate whether your emotional response is justified or if there might be a misunderstanding that requires clarification.

Examples of Emotional Regulation in Challenging Situations

Let's consider a common scenario: a disagreement with a loved one. In the heat of the moment, words are exchanged, and anger starts to simmer. Without emotional self-regulation, this situation can quickly escalate into a full-blown argument.

However, when emotional regulation is applied, the outcome can drastically differ. Instead of reacting impulsively, you pause to take a deep breath, allowing yourself to cool down. You choose to respond thoughtfully, acknowledging the other person's perspective and suggesting a more productive approach to resolving the issue. As a result, what could have been an escalating argument transforms into a constructive conversation.

This chapter will delve into real-life stories of individuals who have harnessed emotional intelligence to transform their lives. These stories are inspiring examples of how emotional self-regulation has not only diffused anger but also fostered personal growth, strengthened relationships, and improved overall well-being.

By honing your skills in managing emotional responses, you benefit yourself and contribute to a more harmonious and compassionate world. Emotional intelligence is a journey of self-discovery and growth. As you navigate its path, you will find yourself better equipped to handle the storms of anger and emerge from them with greater clarity and wisdom.

Communicating Emotions Effectively

Communication is the bridge that connects us to others, allowing us to share our thoughts, feelings, and experiences. However, effective communication is often challenging when it comes to expressing our emotions, especially anger. Here, we will explore the importance of using "I" statements and active listening as key tools for successful emotional communication. Additionally, we'll provide practical dialogue templates and share inspiring case studies of individuals who have mastered the art of expressing their emotions constructively.

The Power of Emotional Communication

Effective communication of emotions is not just about expressing yourself—it's also about being heard and understood. Clear emotional expression can make all the difference, Whether in a personal relationship, at work, or in everyday interactions.

Using "I" Statements

"I" statements is a simple yet powerful way to express your emotions honestly and assertively. They focus on your feelings, needs, and experiences rather than placing blame or making accusatory statements. By using "I" statements, you take ownership of your emotions and create a safe space for open dialogue.

Active Listening: The Other Half of the Equation

While expressing your emotions is important, listening is equally vital in effective emotional communication. Active listening involves giving your full attention to the speaker, suspending judgment, and empathizing with their perspective. It demonstrates respect and validates the emotions of the other person.

Dialogue Templates for Constructive Expression

Expressing Anger: When addressing a situation that has triggered your anger, use a template like: "I felt [emotion] when [specific situation] because it made me feel [impact on you]. I would appreciate [specific request or solution]."

Expressing Hurt or Disappointment: If someone's actions have hurt you, you might say: "I felt hurt when [describe the action] because it made me feel [your emotional response]. I want to understand [seek clarification or express a need]."

Expressing Positive Emotions: Emotional communication is not limited to negative feelings. Share your positive emotions, too! For instance: "I feel grateful for [what you appreciate] because it [impacts on you]. I wanted to tell you how much I value [the person or situation]."

Case Studies of Successful Emotional Communication

Sarah and Mark's Journey: Sarah and Mark, a married couple, struggled with unresolved conflicts and escalating arguments. They decided to attend couples therapy, where they learned about "I" statements and active listening. By applying these techniques, they transformed their communication. Instead of saying, "You always ignore me," Sarah learned to say, "I feel unheard when we don't have time to talk because it's important to me." This shift in communication allowed them to address their needs and concerns constructively, ultimately strengthening their relationship.

<u>John's Office Diplomacy</u>: In a high-stress workplace, John often clashed with his co-workers. After attending a conflict resolution workshop, he used "I" statements to express his frustrations and concerns. Rather than saying, "You're always interrupting my work," he began saying, "I feel distracted and stressed when there are frequent interruptions because it affects my productivity. Can we find a solution together?" John's colleagues appreciated his open communication style, and together, they found ways to create a more productive work environment.

Mastering the art of emotional communication is transformative. It can heal personal relationships wounds, prevent work misunderstandings, and enhance everyday interactions. By embracing "I" statements, active listening, and constructive dialogue templates, you'll find that expressing your emotions becomes a source of connection and understanding rather than conflict and discord.

The Role of Empathy

Empathy, often described as the ability to understand and share the feelings of another, is a powerful tool for managing anger and enhancing emotional intelligence. We will explore the profound impact of empathy on personal and professional relationships. We'll provide exercises to help you develop and express empathy and share inspiring stories of how empathy can lead to resolving anger and conflicts.

The Transformative Power of Empathy

Empathy is the bridge that connects one person's emotional world to another's. It allows us to step into someone else's shoes and see the world from their perspective. This simple act of understanding can be a game-changer in handling anger and conflicts in our lives.

Empathy in Personal Relationships

In personal relationships, empathy plays a critical role in deepening emotional connections and resolving conflicts. When you empathize with your partner, friend, or family member, you create an atmosphere of trust and understanding. You validate their feelings and make them feel heard and valued.

Empathy in Professional Life

Empathy is not limited to personal relationships—it's equally important in the workplace. Colleagues who can empathize with each other are more likely to collaborate effectively, resolve disputes, and foster a positive work environment. Leaders who show empathy better motivate their teams and address employee concerns.

Exercises to Develop and Express Empathy

Active Listening: Practice active listening by giving your full attention to the speaker without interrupting or passing judgment. Try to understand not only the words being said but also the emotions behind them.

Mirror Emotions: When someone shares their feelings with you, try to mirror them in your responses. For example, if they express frustration, you might respond, "I can see why you're frustrated; that sounds challenging."

Ask Open-ended Questions: Encourage others to share their thoughts and emotions by asking open-ended questions. Instead of asking, "Did that upset you?" you can ask, "How did that make you feel?"

Empathy Journal: Keep a journal where you record situations where you successfully empathized with others. Reflect on the impact of your empathy in these situations.

Stories of Empathy Leading to Anger Resolution

Lisa's Family Reunion: Lisa's family had a long history of unresolved conflicts and simmering tensions. At a family reunion, Lisa decided to approach the situation differently. When her cousin, Sam, expressed frustration about their family's inability to communicate, Lisa didn't dismiss his feelings. Instead, she empathized with him, acknowledging the pain he felt. This led to a heartfelt conversation where other family members also shared their emotions. Over time, their family began to heal as empathy opened the door to understanding and forgiveness.

John's Workplace Harmony: John, a manager at a tech company, faced a team struggling with low morale and internal conflicts. Instead of imposing strict rules or reprimanding employees, John took a different approach. He began holding regular one-on-one meetings with his team members, actively listening to their concerns and empathizing with their challenges. This shift in leadership style transformed the team's dynamics. They started working together more cohesively, and productivity soared due to John's empathetic leadership.

Empathy is a skill that can be cultivated and refined. As you develop your capacity for empathy, you'll notice improvements in your personal and professional relationships. Conflict resolution becomes smoother, misunderstandings decrease, and you'll find it easier to manage anger by understanding the emotions of those around you. Ultimately, empathy is a powerful tool for building bridges to understanding and fostering harmonious connections with others.

Building Emotional Resilience

In life's ever-changing landscape, emotional resilience stands as a robust fortress against the storms of stress and anger. Let's go deeper into the strategies for enhancing your emotional resilience, explore the role of positive psychology in this endeavor, and draw inspiration from real-life anecdotes of individuals who have triumphed over adversity through their inner strength.

Emotional resilience is the ability to bounce back from adversity, adapt and grow stronger in the face of life's challenges. The inner fortitude empowers you to withstand stress, manage anger constructively, and maintain emotional well-being.

Strategies for Building Resilience

1. <u>Embrace Change</u>: Resilience begins with acceptance. Understand that change is a constant part of life; sometimes, it's beyond your control. Embracing change as an opportunity for growth can make you more adaptable.

2. <u>Cultivate Optimism</u>: Positive thinking is a cornerstone of resilience. Instead of dwelling on setbacks, focus on the possibilities and opportunities they bring. Optimism can help reframe challenges as stepping stones to success.

3. <u>Nurture Self-Compassion</u>: Treat yourself with kindness and understanding, especially when you face difficulties or make mistakes.

Self-compassion allows you to bounce back faster and with greater resilience.

4. <u>Develop Problem-Solving Skills</u>: Effective problem-solving is a crucial resilience tool. By breaking down problems into manageable steps and seeking solutions, you regain a sense of control over your circumstances.

5. <u>Build a Support Network</u>: Connecting with friends, family, or support groups can provide you with a safety net during tough times. Social support is a vital resource for enhancing resilience.

6. <u>Practice Mindfulness</u>: Mindfulness techniques can help you stay grounded in the present moment, reducing the impact of past regrets or future worries on your emotional well-being.

Positive Psychology and Emotional Resilience

Positive psychology is a branch of psychology that focuses on fostering positive emotions, strengths, and well-being. It plays a pivotal role in building emotional resilience by emphasizing the importance of developing and utilizing your strengths and cultivating a positive outlook on life.

Anecdotes of Triumph over Adversity

<u>Sarah's Story of Loss and Resilience</u>: Sarah, a single mother, faced a devastating job loss during a recession. This sudden upheaval threatened her financial stability and put her under immense stress. However, Sarah refused to succumb to despair. Instead, she used this time to explore new career opportunities and sharpen her skills. Her emotional resilience enabled her to secure a better job and inspire her children with her unwavering determination to overcome adversity.

<u>David's Journey through Grief</u>: David lost his wife to a terminal illness, plunging him into a deep well of grief and anger. With the help of therapy and the support of friends, he navigated the complex emotions that accompanied his loss. Through his journey, David learned that grieving was a natural process, and he gradually developed emotional resilience. He now channels his experiences into supporting others facing similar challenges, emphasizing the importance of emotional strength in times of sorrow.

Building emotional resilience is a lifelong journey that involves nurturing your mental and emotional well-being. By embracing change, cultivating optimism, practicing self-compassion, developing problem-solving skills, and seeking support, you can fortify your inner strength to manage anger better, overcome adversity, and thrive in all aspects of life. Remember, your resilience is your greatest asset in the face of life's uncertainties.

Chapter Seven

Lifestyle Adjustments for Anger Control

In the hustle and bustle of our daily lives, anger often creeps in like an uninvited guest, disrupting our peace and leaving us with a trail of emotional debris. Have you ever found yourself fuming in traffic, simmering over a misunderstood text message, or exploding over seemingly trivial matters? If you're nodding your head in recognition, you're not alone. Anger is a universal emotion, and we all experience it occasionally. But what if I told you that there are lifestyle adjustments you can make to take charge of your anger and find a path to lasting change? Let me take you on a journey to explore the transformative power of lifestyle adjustments, where we will weave together personal anecdotes, practical advice, and a roadmap to a more balanced, anger-free life.

Before we dive into the heart of this chapter, allow me to share a personal story that led me to write about the importance of lifestyle adjustments in managing anger.

Picture this: I was caught in a never-ending cycle of work-related stress, deadlines that seemed to multiply like rabbits, and a demanding daily routine that left me exhausted and perpetually on edge. My journey with anger was akin to an unwelcome shadow, following me through the day and casting a gloom over my interactions with loved ones. Arguments that seemed to come out of nowhere, sleepless nights spent mulling over frustrations, and a growing sense of helplessness painted a grim picture.

During one particularly heated exchange with a dear friend, I realized something had to change. Once spoken in the heat of the moment, words can leave lasting scars. I decided to embark on a personal transformation, seeking out methods and strategies to rein in my anger and regain control over my life. It was through this journey that I discovered the profound impact of lifestyle adjustments in curbing anger's destructive force.

You might be wondering why this chapter on lifestyle adjustments matters in your quest for anger control. The answer is simple: change begins with you and starts with how you live your life. By understanding the intricate dance between your daily choices and your emotional state, you can take proactive steps toward a more balanced, anger-free existence.

In the following pages, you'll uncover the benefits of lifestyle adjustments extending far beyond anger management. We'll explore how your daily routines, habits, and choices can influence your emotional well-being, relationships, and overall quality of life. Whether it's through mindful living, stress reduction, healthy communication, or nurturing your physical and mental health, these lifestyle adjustments hold the key to unlocking the peaceful, harmonious life you deserve.

By the end of this chapter, you'll have a deeper understanding of:

- The Interplay Between Lifestyle and Anger: Explore how your daily choices can either fuel or quell anger.

- Practical Strategies for Lifestyle Adjustments: Discover actionable steps to make meaningful changes in your life.

- Benefits Beyond Anger Control: Learn how these adjustments can enhance your overall well-being and relationships.

- Your Personal Journey: Embark on a transformative path toward lasting change, just as I did.

So, my fellow traveler on the road to anger control, let's embark on this adventure together. By the time you turn the final page of this chapter, you'll be armed with valuable insights and practical tools to pave the way for a more serene and fulfilling life. It's time to embrace the power of lifestyle adjustments and reclaim the tranquility that anger often steals from us.

Diet and Anger

In our journey toward mastering anger control, we've explored various techniques and strategies to tame the flames of our temper. But what if I told you that the key to managing anger effectively might also be found on your plate? Yes, you read that correctly – your diet plays a crucial role in influencing your mood and, consequently, your anger. Welcome to this part where we'll delve into the fascinating connection between what you eat and how you feel and discover how dietary choices can significantly impact your emotional well-being.

Before we dig deeper into the specifics of diet and its effect on anger, let's take a moment to consider how our food choices can influence our emotions. We've all experienced it – the post-sugar crash after indulging in a sugary treat or the sluggish, heavy feeling that follows a big, greasy meal. These are just a couple of examples of daily nutritional mood swings.

But it goes beyond that. Emerging research suggests that the foods we consume on a regular basis can have a profound impact on our emotional health, including how we manage anger. Our dietary habits can either fan the flames of frustration or act as a soothing balm to calm our inner turmoil.

The Diet-Mood Connection

So, what is the connection between diet and mood? Simply put, the food you eat directly influences the chemicals and neurotransmitters in your brain, which, in turn, affect your emotions. Let's explore this connection in more detail:

1. <u>Blood Sugar Balance</u>: When you consume foods high in refined sugars and carbohydrates, your blood sugar levels can spike and crash rapidly. This rollercoaster ride can lead to irritability, mood swings, and even anger.

2. <u>Brain Chemicals</u>: Certain nutrients found in foods play a role in the production of brain chemicals like serotonin and dopamine, which

are vital for regulating mood. For example, tryptophan, an amino acid found in turkey and nuts, is a precursor to serotonin, the "feel-good" neurotransmitter.

3. <u>Gut-Brain Axis</u>: Emerging research on the gut-brain connection suggests that the state of your gut microbiome can influence your mood. A healthy gut promotes emotional balance, while an imbalanced one can contribute to feelings of anxiety and anger.

4. <u>Inflammation</u>: Chronic inflammation, often driven by a poor diet, has been linked to mood disorders, including irritability and aggression. Foods high in antioxidants and anti-inflammatory compounds can help mitigate this.

A Diet for Emotional Balance

Now that we understand the link between diet and mood, let's explore what a diet for emotional balance looks like:

1. <u>Complex Carbohydrates</u>: Opt for complex carbohydrates like whole grains, fruits, and vegetables. These release energy slowly, providing a stable fuel source for your brain and reducing mood swings.

2. <u>Lean Proteins</u>: Include lean protein sources such as poultry, fish, beans, and tofu. They provide the amino acids necessary for neurotransmitter production.

3. <u>Healthy Fats</u>: Incorporate sources of healthy fats like avocados, nuts, seeds, and olive oil. Omega-3 fatty acids, in particular, are known for their mood-stabilizing properties.

4. <u>Mood-Boosting Nutrients</u>: Prioritize foods rich in mood-boosting nutrients, such as tryptophan, magnesium, and B vitamins. Examples include turkey, spinach, and whole grains.

5. <u>Probiotic-Rich Foods</u>: Support your gut health with probiotic-rich foods like yogurt, kefir, and fermented vegetables. A happy gut often translates to a happier mood.

6. <u>Hydration</u>: Stay adequately hydrated by drinking enough water throughout the day. Dehydration can lead to irritability and exacerbate anger.

Recipes and Meal Plans

As a bonus, I've included a collection of recipes and meal plans designed to support emotional balance and anger control. These recipes feature ingredients known for their mood-enhancing properties, and the meal plans offer a balanced approach to nutrition that can help stabilize your emotions.

<u>Serotonin-Boosting Smoothie</u>: A delicious blend of banana, Greek yogurt, and walnuts to elevate your serotonin levels.

<u>Salmon and Quinoa Bowl</u>: Packed with omega-3s and protein, this meal promotes a stable mood.

<u>Mood-Enhancing Salad</u>: A colorful mix of leafy greens, berries, and nuts rich in antioxidants and nutrients.

<u>Anti-Inflammatory Stir-Fry</u>: A tasty stir-fry loaded with vegetables, tofu, and turmeric for inflammation control.

<u>Gut-Healing Breakfast</u>: A probiotic-rich breakfast bowl featuring yogurt, granola, and fermented fruits.

As we conclude this diet exploration and its profound impact on anger and emotional well-being, remember that making conscious dietary choices is just one piece of the puzzle. Alongside diet, other lifestyle adjustments, as discussed in this chapter, play crucial roles in managing anger effectively. By nurturing your body and mind through mindful eating, you're taking significant steps toward emotional balance and a life where anger no longer holds the reins. So, let's embark on this journey to harness the power of food and cultivate a more serene and composed you.

Exercise as an Outlet

Imagine a pressure cooker, its lid tightly sealed, steam hissing, and pressure building with each passing moment. If there's no release valve, it's only a matter of time before it explodes. Much like this pressure cooker, our bodies can build up stress and anger, requiring a healthy outlet to prevent an emotional explosion. Now, it's time to explore the transformative power of exercise as an outlet for managing anger.

The Anger-Exercise Connection

The relationship between exercise and anger management is not just a coincidence; it's deeply rooted in science. When you engage in physical activity, your body releases a surge of neurochemicals and hormones that can profoundly calm your mind and emotions. Here's how it works:

1. <u>Mood-Boosting Neurotransmitters</u>: Exercise stimulates the production of mood-enhancing neurotransmitters like serotonin and endorphins. These natural chemicals are often referred to as "feel-good" substances because they can elevate your mood and reduce feelings of anger and irritability.

2. <u>Stress Reduction</u>: Physical activity triggers the release of stress-reducing hormones, such as cortisol. These hormones help your body manage and cope with stressors, preventing them from snowballing into anger.

3. <u>Energy Release</u>: Engaging in vigorous exercise provides an outlet for pent-up energy, frustration, and restlessness. This physical release can help you feel more relaxed and less agitated.

4. <u>Improved Sleep</u>: Regular exercise can improve the quality and duration of your sleep, which, in turn, can reduce irritability and make it easier to manage anger.

Creating Your Personal Exercise Routine

Now that we've established the positive impact of exercise on anger management, let's explore how you can create a personalized exercise routine tailored to your needs:

1. <u>Identify Your Preferences</u>: Start by identifying activities you enjoy. Whether it's jogging, swimming, dancing, or playing a sport, choosing something you love will increase your motivation to stick with it.

2. <u>Set Realistic Goals</u>: Define clear and achievable exercise goals. Are you seeking to reduce stress, improve your mood, or enhance your fitness? Setting specific objectives will guide your routine.

3. <u>Schedule Regular Sessions</u>: Consistency is key in reaping the emotional benefits of exercise. Create a weekly schedule that includes dedicated time for physical activity.

4. <u>Mix It Up</u>: Variety can keep your exercise routine exciting. Incorporate different types of workouts to prevent boredom and ensure a well-rounded fitness regimen.

5. <u>Start Slowly</u>: If you're new to exercise or haven't been active for a while, start slowly and gradually increase the intensity and duration of your workouts to avoid injury.

Success Stories of Exercise and Anger Transformation

To further illustrate the power of exercise in anger management, let's explore a few success stories:

Case Study 1: <u>Sarah's Stress-Relieving Yoga</u>

Sarah, a busy professional, found herself frequently succumbing to anger and frustration due to her demanding job. She decided to try yoga as a means of relaxation. Over time, the practice of mindful stretching and controlled breathing helped her stay composed, even in high-pressure situations.

Case Study 2: <u>John's Running Journey</u>

John, a middle-aged father of two, struggled with anger issues stemming from work-related stress and family responsibilities. He took up running as an outlet, and the daily jogs allowed him to release tension and reflect on his emotions. As his physical health improved, so did his emotional well-being.

Case Study 3: <u>Maria's Kickboxing Adventure</u>

Maria, a young student, had difficulty managing her anger and impulsive reactions. She joined a kickboxing class, which provided a structured environment for releasing her pent-up frustration. Through discipline and self-control learned in class, Maria gained a new perspective on handling anger outside of it.

Exercise isn't just about building a stronger body; it's about cultivating emotional resilience and providing an outlet for anger and stress. Integrating physical activity into your daily routine can harness its incredible potential to transform anger into positive energy, leaving you feeling more centered, composed, and in control of your emotions. So, let's lace up those sneakers, dive into your favorite activity, and unlock the power of exercise on your journey towards anger control.

The Impact of Sleep

Picture a day when you wake up after a full night's sleep, feeling refreshed, alert, and ready to take on the world. Now contrast that with a night when sleep eluded you, leaving you groggy, irritable, and quick to anger. It's a familiar scenario for many of us. Let's study the relationship between sleep and anger, explore the science behind it, and provide you with practical tips to enhance your sleep quality for better anger control.

Unpacking the Sleep-Anger Connection

Sleep is often called the "reset button" for our minds and emotions. It plays a pivotal role in regulating our mood, managing stress, and maintaining emotional equilibrium. When we experience inadequate or poor-quality sleep, our emotional well-being can take a hit, making us more prone to anger and irritability. Here's why:

1. <u>Emotional Resilience</u>: During deep sleep, the brain processes and consolidates emotions from the day. It helps us make sense of our feelings, allowing us to wake up with a fresh emotional perspective. When deprived of this crucial process, we may carry unresolved emotional baggage into our waking hours, increasing the likelihood of emotional outbursts.

2. <u>Stress Hormones</u>: Sleep deprivation triggers the release of stress hormones like cortisol. Elevated cortisol levels are associated with heightened emotional reactivity, making it more challenging to manage anger and frustration.

3. <u>Impaired Cognitive Function</u>: Poor sleep impairs cognitive functions such as decision-making, problem-solving, and impulse control. When we're sleep-deprived, our ability to think rationally and respond calmly to triggers diminishes, leading to impulsive anger responses.

4. <u>Reduced Patience</u>: A lack of sleep can reduce our patience and tolerance for frustration. Minor annoyances that we might usually brush off can escalate into significant sources of anger.

Tips for Improving Sleep Quality

The good news is that you can take concrete steps to improve your sleep quality and, in turn, enhance your ability to manage anger. Here are some valuable tips:

1. <u>Prioritize Consistency</u>: Establish a regular sleep schedule by going to bed and waking up at the same times each day, even on weekends. This consistency helps regulate your body's internal clock.

2. <u>Create a Relaxing Bedtime Routine</u>: Engage in calming activities before bedtime, such as reading a book, taking a warm bath, or practicing relaxation techniques. These rituals signal to your body that it's time to wind down.

3. <u>Optimize Sleep Environment</u>: Ensure your bedroom is conducive to sleep by keeping it dark, cool, and quiet. Invest in a comfortable mattress and pillows for optimal comfort.

4. <u>Limit Screen Time</u>: The blue light emitted by screens can interfere with producing the sleep hormone melatonin. Aim to avoid screens for at least an hour before bedtime.

5. <u>Watch Your Diet</u>: Avoid heavy or spicy meals close to bedtime, as they can disrupt sleep. Additionally, limit caffeine and alcohol intake, especially in the evening.

6. <u>Stay Active</u>: Regular physical activity can promote better sleep, but try to avoid intense workouts close to bedtime.

The Science Behind Sleep and Anger Regulation

Numerous studies have explored the intricate relationship between sleep and emotional regulation. One particularly relevant study published in the Journal of Sleep Research found that even a single night of sleep deprivation can increase emotional reactivity, particularly to anger-inducing stimuli. Another study in the journal Sleep Medicine Reviews revealed that individuals with chronic sleep disturbances are more likely to experience intense anger and irritability.

These findings underscore the importance of quality sleep in maintaining emotional balance. By prioritizing your sleep and adopting healthy sleep habits, you can fortify your emotional resilience and significantly reduce your susceptibility to anger outbursts.

Sleep is not just a biological necessity; it's a powerful tool for managing anger and enhancing emotional regulation. The profound impact of sleep on our mood, stress levels, and cognitive functioning cannot be overstated. By recognizing the connection between sleep and anger and by implementing strategies to improve your sleep quality, you can take a significant step toward better anger control and emotional well-being. So, let's set the stage for restorative sleep and wake up to more composed, emotionally balanced days ahead.

Time Management and Stress Reduction

Imagine this: You're rushing through a chaotic morning, trying to get yourself ready for work, pack lunch for your kids, respond to a barrage of emails, and prepare for a crucial meeting—all before 9 a.m. Sound familiar? In today's fast-paced world, time management and stress reduction have become essential skills for maintaining our sanity and controlling anger. We'll take a look at the intricate relationship between time management, stress, and anger and provide you with practical strategies to help you regain control of your time and emotions.

The Time-Stress-Anger Connection

Time management isn't just about getting more done in less time; it's about achieving a sense of control and reducing the stress that can fuel anger. Here's how the pieces fit together:

1. <u>Stress and Anger</u>: When we're overwhelmed with too many tasks and not enough time, stress levels rise. This heightened stress can prime us for anger, making us more irritable, impatient, and prone to emotional outbursts.

2. <u>Lack of Control</u>: Feeling constantly rushed and overwhelmed can create a sense of powerlessness, which can significantly trigger anger. We might lash out at others or react angrily to minor frustrations because we feel like we've lost control of our time.

3. <u>Impaired Decision-Making</u>: Stress impairs our cognitive abilities, including decision-making and impulse control. When we're stressed due to poor time management, we're more likely to make hasty and regrettable decisions in the heat of the moment.

Strategies for Effective Time Management and Stress Reduction

1. <u>Prioritize Tasks</u>: Start by identifying your most important and urgent tasks. Use tools like the Eisenhower Matrix to categorize tasks as urgent/important, not urgent/important, urgent/not important, or neither. Focus your energy on what falls into the urgent/important quadrant.

2. <u>Set SMART Goals</u>: SMART goals are Specific, Measurable, Achievable, Relevant, and Time-bound. They provide a clear framework for setting and achieving your objectives, reducing ambiguity and stress.

3. <u>Time Blocking</u>: Allocate specific blocks of time for different tasks or activities. This approach helps you concentrate on one task at a time rather than constantly switching between them.

4. <u>Delegate When Possible</u>: Don't be afraid to delegate tasks that others can handle. Delegation reduces your workload and empowers others, freeing up your time and reducing stress.

5. <u>Learn to Say No</u>: Politely decline additional commitments or tasks that you don't have the bandwidth to handle. Saying no is a vital skill for maintaining boundaries and managing stress.

6. <u>Avoid Multitasking</u>: Contrary to popular belief, multitasking often reduces productivity and increases stress. Focus on one task at a time to achieve better results.

7. <u>Practice Mindfulness</u>: Incorporate mindfulness techniques into your daily routine to reduce stress and enhance your ability to manage your reactions to challenging situations.

Real-Life Impact of Effective Time Management

Consider the following scenario: Sarah, a busy working mother, often finds herself overwhelmed by her daily responsibilities. Her mornings were chaotic, leading to frequent arguments with her children and husband. She realized that her lack of time management was taking a toll on her relationships and her well-being.

Sarah decided to implement some of the strategies mentioned above. She began waking up 30 minutes earlier to create a calm morning routine, setting aside time for meditation and planning her day. She regained control over her schedule by prioritizing tasks, delegating chores, and saying no to additional commitments.

The results were remarkable. Sarah's stress levels decreased significantly, and her relationships improved due to reduced tension in the household. She noticed that she was less prone to anger and better equipped to handle challenges that came her way.

Effective time management isn't just about squeezing more tasks into your day; it's about reclaiming control over your life and reducing the stress that can fuel anger. You can regain a sense of equilibrium and emotional control by prioritizing tasks, setting clear goals, and implementing stress-reduction techniques. So, take charge of your time, and you'll find yourself better equipped to manage anger and embrace a more peaceful, balanced life.

Hobbies and Relaxation

In the hustle and bustle of our daily lives, it's easy to get caught up in the demands of work, family, and other obligations. The never-ending to-do lists and constant juggling of responsibilities can leave us feeling stressed, overwhelmed, and sometimes teetering on the brink of anger. That's where the beauty of hobbies and relaxation comes into play, offering us a much-needed escape and a pathway to emotional balance.

The Healing Power of Hobbies

Imagine this: You're engrossed in painting a vivid landscape, strumming your guitar, or tending to a flourishing garden. The outside world fades away in these moments, and your mind is immersed in the present, free from worries and frustrations. Hobbies uniquely transport us to a state of flow, where time seems to stand still and stress melts away.

1. <u>Stress Reduction</u>: Engaging in hobbies triggers the relaxation response in our bodies, reducing the production of stress hormones like

cortisol. This leads to a sense of calm and tranquility that counteracts the buildup of anger.

2. <u>Emotional Release</u>: Hobbies provide a healthy outlet for our emotions. Instead of bottling up anger, we can channel it into creative or physical activities, releasing tension and frustration constructively.

3. <u>Improved Mood</u>: The pleasure and satisfaction derived from pursuing hobbies lead to an improved mood and increased feelings of happiness. When we're happier, we're less likely to succumb to anger.

Suggestions for Anger-Management Hobbies

Here are some hobbies that have proven effective in helping individuals manage anger:

1. <u>Artistic Pursuits</u>: Painting, drawing, sculpting, or any form of creative expression can be incredibly therapeutic. It allows you to channel your emotions into art and create something beautiful in the process.

2. <u>Music</u>: Playing a musical instrument or simply listening to music can soothe the soul and provide an emotional release. The act of making music or immersing yourself in its melodies can be a powerful anger management tool.

3. <u>Gardening</u>: Tending to plants and nurturing a garden provides a sense of accomplishment and connection with nature. It's a peaceful, meditative activity that calms the mind and reduces stress.

4. <u>Physical Activities</u>: Engaging in sports, yoga, or other physical activities helps release built-up tension. Exercise triggers the release of endorphins, which are natural mood lifters.

5. <u>Writing:</u> Journaling, creative writing, or blogging allows you to express your thoughts and emotions in a safe space. Writing can be a therapeutic way to process anger and gain insight into your feelings.

Personal Stories of Hobbies as Emotional Release

Let's delve into a couple of personal stories to illustrate how hobbies can serve as powerful tools for anger management:

1. <u>Susan's Painting Journey</u>: Susan had a demanding job in the corporate world that often left her feeling stressed and irritable. One day, she decided to take up painting as a hobby. As she dipped her brush into vibrant colors and let her emotions flow onto the canvas, she discovered a newfound sense of serenity. Painting became her refuge, a place where she could release pent-up anger and transform it into art. Over time, her anger diminished, and her creativity flourished.

2. <u>Mike's Guitar Solace</u>: Mike struggled with anger issues that strained his relationships. He turned to playing the guitar as a form of relaxation. Whenever he felt the familiar surge of anger, he would pick up his guitar and pour his emotions into the music. The melodies he created acted as a soothing balm for his soul. Gradually, his anger became less frequent and less intense, and his loved ones noticed a positive change in his temperament.

Hobbies and relaxation are not just leisure activities but essential tools for maintaining emotional balance and managing anger. By immersing yourself in creative or physical pursuits that bring you joy and peace, you can release tension, reduce stress, and improve your overall mood. Whether it's painting, playing an instrument, gardening, or any other hobby, finding time for these activities can help you find the equilibrium needed to navigate life's challenges with a calmer, more composed demeanor.

Chapter Eight
Anger in Relationships

As the sun dipped below the horizon, casting a warm, golden hue across the tranquil lake, I found myself reminiscing about a vivid memory from my past. It was a memory etched with laughter and frustration, a testament to the intricacies of human relationships and the formidable force of anger.

It was a lazy Sunday afternoon, and my friend Alex and I had embarked on an adventure that involved assembling a piece of furniture. Armed with a jigsaw puzzle of wooden panels, bolts, and an instruction manual that resembled hieroglyphics, we were ready to tackle the challenge. Little did we know that our quest for DIY glory would soon turn into a comical display of anger management—or the lack thereof.

Our journey began with enthusiasm and a sense of camaraderie. We unfolded the instruction manual and studied it intently, confident that we could decipher its cryptic symbols. But as the hours passed, our optimism waned, and frustration crept in. The once-clear instructions became increasingly ambiguous, leading to countless mismatches and perplexing configurations.

As the project unfolded, so did our tempers. Our exchanges transformed from cheerful banter to heated debates about the correct placement of a wooden beam or the purpose of an enigmatic screw. Frustration gave way to annoyance, and annoyance escalated into anger. At one point, I believe we were both convinced that the other was intentionally trying to sabotage our mission.

After a series of exasperated sighs, passionate gestures, and not-so-subtle name-calling, we found ourselves in a standoff. The incomplete piece of furniture loomed ominously in the background, a testament to our shared frustration. It was then that we realized the futility of our anger. We were not adversaries; we were friends on a mission.

With that realization, we took a step back, shared a moment of laughter at our own expense, and decided to approach the situation differently. We acknowledged that our anger was not helping us solve the problem but hindering us. To our amazement, we chose patience over impatience, collaboration over conflict, and successfully completed the furniture assembly.

This chapter, "Anger in Relationships," delves into the complex interplay of emotions, communication, and human connection within the realm of anger. It is a chapter born from personal experiences like the one I just shared, experiences that revealed the destructive potential of anger within relationships, and the transformative power of effective anger management.

In this chapter, we explore the profound impact of anger on our interactions with those we hold dear—our partners, family members, friends, and colleagues. We dissect the anatomy of anger in relationships, shedding light on why it arises, how it manifests, and the toll it can take on our bonds.

We delve into the intricate dynamics of communication during moments of anger, where words become weapons or tools for resolution. We examine the role of empathy, active listening, and emotional intelligence in defusing anger's ticking time bombs.

But more than just understanding the challenges anger poses in our relationships, this chapter offers hope and guidance. It provides practical strategies for conflict resolution, effective communication, and rebuilding trust when anger has left its mark. It empowers you to navigate the stormy seas of anger within relationships with compassion, empathy, and a shared commitment to growth.

As you journey through the pages of this chapter, you will:

- Gain insights into the common triggers of anger within relationships and how to identify them.

- Discover effective communication techniques that can defuse tense situations and foster understanding.

- Explore the power of empathy in bridging gaps and healing emotional wounds.

- Find strategies for rebuilding trust and repairing relationships strained by anger.

- In Conclusion

This chapter is your compass for steering through the tempestuous waters of anger within your relationships. By embracing the wisdom within these pages, you will be better equipped to transform moments of anger into opportunities for growth, connection, and lasting harmony. So, let's embark on this enlightening journey together as we explore the fascinating world of anger in relationships and learn how to navigate it with grace and resilience.

The Dynamics of Anger in Relationships

Anger, like a tempestuous wind, can sweep through our lives, leaving behind a trail of debris and discord. Nowhere is this more evident than within our relationships. Whether it's a romantic partnership, familial bonds, friendships, or professional associations, the dynamics of anger can profoundly impact the health and longevity of these connections.

We'll explore how anger manifests within various types of relationships, the cyclic nature of anger and conflict, and the eye-opening statistics illuminating the real-world consequences of unchecked anger on the health of our relationships.

Anger's Reach Across Relationships

Anger doesn't discriminate; it infiltrates every facet of our lives, seeping into our most cherished relationships. Let's take a closer look at how anger can affect different types of relationships:

Romantic Relationships: In the realm of romantic partnerships, anger can be both a test of love's endurance and a catalyst for growth. Intimate relationships often provide the ideal breeding ground for anger to emerge due to their depth of emotional involvement. Unresolved anger can fester, leading to resentment and a chasm in communication. However, when managed effectively, anger can pave the way for deeper intimacy as couples learn to understand and support each other in navigating life's challenges.

Family Bonds: Family relationships are not immune to the influence of anger. Sibling rivalries, parent-child conflicts, and disagreements among extended family members can all ignite the flames of anger. The dynamics of power, authority, and long-held roles can complicate the expression and resolution of anger within families.

Friendships: Even the closest of friendships are not exempt from anger's occasional visit. Misunderstandings, betrayals, or divergent life paths can stir feelings of anger among friends. How these emotions are managed can either fortify or fracture the bonds of friendship.

Professional Associations: In the workplace, anger can create tension, disrupt teamwork, and hinder career advancement. Conflicts between colleagues, supervisors, or subordinates can lead to a hostile work environment if anger is left unaddressed. On the other hand, effectively managing anger can lead to constructive problem-solving and professional growth.

The Cycle of Anger and Conflict

Anger has an inherent cyclical nature within relationships. When unmanaged, it can perpetuate a destructive cycle that goes something like this:

Trigger: An event or circumstance triggers anger within one or more parties involved. This trigger can range from a perceived injustice to a simple misunderstanding.

Reaction: Anger prompts a visceral reaction—a surge of adrenaline, a racing heart, and a desire to retaliate or defend oneself. This emotional response often leads to heated arguments, blame-shifting, or withdrawal.

Conflict: The reaction of anger from one party elicits a response from the other(s), perpetuating the conflict. The anger cycle can intensify as both parties become entrenched in their positions, often escalating the situation further.

Repercussions: The conflict can have significant repercussions, such as emotional scars, damaged trust, or strained relationships. In extreme cases, it can lead to separation or estrangement.

Statistics on the Impact of Anger on Relationship Health

To truly understand the gravity of anger's impact on relationships, consider these statistics:

In a study conducted by the American Psychological Association, nearly half of all adults reported losing patience, yelling, or becoming angry with their partner at least once a month.

Research published in the journal "Psychological Science" found that couples who engaged in angry, hostile interactions had higher levels of inflammation, which is associated with chronic illnesses like heart disease and cancer.

According to a survey by Mental Health America, 60% of respondents reported that their partner's anger or emotional abuse had a significant impact on their mental health.

These statistics underscore the pervasive and potentially devastating effects of unmanaged anger on the health and well-being of our relationships.

Anger is a potent force that permeates our relationships, impacting partners, family members, friends, and colleagues alike. Understanding the dynamics of anger within various relationship types, recognizing the cyclic nature of anger and conflict, and acknowledging the sobering statistics that reflect the consequences of uncontrolled anger are essential steps toward healthier, more fulfilling connections.

In the following sections of this chapter, we'll delve deeper into strategies for managing anger within relationships, exploring effective communication, conflict resolution, and rebuilding trust when anger has taken its toll. By understanding anger's dynamics and consequences, we can empower ourselves to transform moments of anger into opportunities for growth, empathy, and lasting harmony in our relationships.

Communication Skills for Conflict Resolution

In the tumultuous sea of human relationships, conflicts are bound to arise. Whether it's a disagreement with your partner, a dispute within your family, a falling out with a friend or tension with a colleague, navigating and resolving conflicts is crucial for maintaining healthy and harmonious connections. This will serve as your compass, guiding you through the waters of effective communication strategies that can help you steer your relationships away from the rocky shores of anger and conflict.

The Power of Effective Communication

Effective communication is the lifeblood of any successful relationship. It allows us to express our thoughts, feelings and needs while also understanding those of others. Strong communication skills can mean the difference between resolution and escalation when conflicts arise.

Here are some essential communication strategies for resolving conflicts:

1. <u>Active Listening</u>: One of the most fundamental aspects of effective communication is active listening. This means not just hearing the words being spoken but truly understanding the message behind them. When engaged in a conflict, consciously listen attentively to the other person without interrupting. Let them express their thoughts and feelings completely before responding.

2. <u>"I" Statements</u>: "I" statements are a powerful tool for expressing your feelings and needs without blaming or accusing others. Instead of saying, "You always do this," try saying, "I feel upset when this happens because it makes me feel unheard." This shift in language can make a world of difference in how your message is received.

3. <u>Stay Calm and Collected</u>: Conflict can be emotionally charged, but it's essential to remain calm and collected during discussions. When emotions run high, take a deep breath and try to regulate your emotional responses. This helps you think more clearly and sets a positive tone for the conversation.

4. <u>Avoid Blame and Accusations</u>: Blame and accusations can quickly derail a conversation. Instead of saying, "You're always so thoughtless," try expressing your feelings and needs: "I feel hurt when I perceive that my needs are not considered."

5. <u>Use "We" Language</u>: In situations where you're working towards a resolution together, employ "we" language to convey that you're both on the same team. For example, say, "How can we find a solution to this issue?" This fosters a sense of collaboration.

6. <u>Empathize and Validate</u>: Acknowledge the other person's feelings and perspective, even if you disagree with them. Empathizing and validating their emotions can help defuse tension and create a more open atmosphere for problem-solving.

7. <u>Seek to Understand</u>: Ask open-ended questions to better understand the other person's point of view. Encourage them to share their thoughts and feelings and be genuinely curious about their perspective.

Role-Playing Exercises for Practice

Effective communication is a skill that can be honed through practice. Here are some role-playing exercises you can try to improve your conflict resolution skills:

Exercise 1: <u>The Active Listener</u>: Find a partner and take turns discussing a recent conflict you've experienced. One person plays the role of the active listener, employing active listening techniques such as nodding, paraphrasing, and asking clarifying questions. Switch roles and discuss another conflict.

Exercise 2: <u>"I" Statements</u>: Write down a list of common conflict scenarios and practice expressing your feelings and needs using "I" statements. For example, "I felt frustrated when you canceled our plans without letting me know in advance because I had made arrangements."

Exercise 3: Role Reversal: In pairs, each person takes turns portraying the other person's perspective in a recent conflict. This exercise can help you understand the other person's feelings and motivations.

Exercise 4: Solution-Oriented Conversations: Practice having conversations focusing on finding solutions rather than dwelling on the problem. Identify a recent conflict and work together to brainstorm potential solutions.

Exercise 5: Empathy and Validation: In pairs, one person shares a recent conflict, and the other person practices empathizing and validating their feelings. The goal is to make the person feel heard and understood.

Conflict is a natural part of relationships but doesn't have to be a destructive force. Effective communication skills can transform conflicts into opportunities for understanding, growth, and resolution. By actively listening, using "I" statements, staying calm, and empathizing with the other person, you can navigate the waters of conflict more effectively. These strategies can help you steer your relationships towards healthier and more harmonious shores, where anger and discord are replaced by understanding and connection.

Setting Boundaries

In the intricate dance of human relationships, boundaries are the invisible lines defining the limits of acceptable and comfort. They serve as the framework for healthy interactions, helping us maintain our emotional well-being and protect our individuality. Understanding the importance of setting and maintaining boundaries is crucial in managing anger within relationships. Now, we'll explore the significance of boundaries, guide you through the process of establishing and maintaining them, and share real-life examples of how boundaries can lead to healthier and more harmonious connections.

The Importance of Setting Healthy Boundaries

Imagine a garden without a fence—beautiful flowers and thriving plants might get trampled, and unwanted pests could invade. Just as a garden needs boundaries to flourish, so do relationships. Healthy boundaries provide structure, safety, and a clear understanding of what is acceptable and what is not. They create a sense of order and mutual respect, fostering an environment where both parties can thrive.

Here's why setting healthy boundaries is essential:

1. <u>Self-Respect</u>: Boundaries express self-respect. When you set boundaries, you communicate your worth and value in a relationship. This self-assuredness can deter others from overstepping or disrespecting your limits.

2. <u>Emotional Well-Being</u>: Boundaries help protect your emotional well-being. They prevent you from being drawn into situations that trigger anger or discomfort. You can avoid becoming entangled in toxic or emotionally draining interactions by defining your limits.

3. <u>Improved Communication</u>: Clear boundaries enhance communication. When both parties understand and respect each other's limits, misunderstandings and conflicts decrease, leading to more constructive and peaceful relationships.

4. <u>Empowerment</u>: Establishing boundaries empowers you to make choices that align with your values and needs. It allows you to prioritize self-care and maintain a sense of control over your life.

5. <u>Mutual Respect</u>: Healthy boundaries foster mutual respect within relationships. They create a space where both individuals feel valued and acknowledged, leading to greater trust and intimacy.

Establishing and Maintaining Boundaries

Setting and maintaining boundaries can be challenging, especially if you've never done it before. However, it's a crucial skill for managing anger within relationships. Here's a step-by-step guide to help you navigate this process:

1. <u>Self-Reflection</u>: Begin by reflecting on your own needs, values, and limits. What makes you uncomfortable? What are your non-negotiables in a relationship? Self-awareness is the foundation of setting boundaries.

2. <u>Identify Boundaries</u>: Identify the specific boundaries you want to establish. These could range from personal space and privacy boundaries to emotional and time-related boundaries. Consider your own needs and what you feel is essential for a healthy relationship.

3. <u>Communicate Clearly</u>: When you're ready to set boundaries, communicate them clearly and assertively. Use "I" statements to express your needs and feelings. For example, say, "I need some alone time to recharge after work," instead of, "You always smother me when I get home."

4. <u>Be Consistent</u>: Consistency is key to maintaining boundaries. Once you've set them, enforce them consistently. Don't waver or compromise on boundaries that are essential to your well-being.

5. <u>Respect Others' Boundaries</u>: Just as you expect others to respect your boundaries, be sure to respect theirs. This reciprocity fosters mutual understanding and cooperation.

6. <u>Adjust as Needed</u>: You may find that your boundaries need adjustment over time. As your relationships evolve or your needs change, revisiting and modifying your boundaries is okay.

Examples of Boundaries Leading to Healthier Relationships

To illustrate the transformative power of healthy boundaries, let's explore a few real-life examples:

1. <u>Work-Life Balance</u>: Sarah struggled with balancing her demanding job with her personal life. She set a boundary by designating specific evenings for quality time with her family. As a result, her relationships with her spouse and children improved, and her stress levels decreased.

2. <u>Emotional Boundaries</u>: John had a friend who constantly shared their personal problems and expected him to provide solutions. John established an emotional boundary by saying, "I care about you, but I can't be your therapist. Let's focus on positive and enjoyable conversations." This boundary preserved their friendship and reduced John's frustration.

3. <u>Personal Space</u>: Maria and her partner decided to create individual spaces within their home. Each person had a designated area to unwind and have alone time. This boundary enhanced their connection

by allowing them to appreciate each other's company without feeling suffocated.

4. <u>Social Media Boundaries</u>: Jake felt overwhelmed by the constant stream of notifications on his phone. He set a boundary by silencing notifications during work hours and dedicating specific times to checking social media. This boundary increased his productivity and reduced his irritability.

Healthy boundaries are the linchpin of harmonious relationships and effective anger management. By understanding their importance, learning how to establish and communicate them, and witnessing their positive impact on real-life relationships, you'll be better equipped to navigate the complex terrain of human connections. Setting boundaries is an act of self-care and self-respect that can lead to more peaceful and fulfilling relationships.

Forgiveness and Letting Go

In the intricate tapestry of human relationships, anger, and hurt are threads that can weave a web of resentment and bitterness. When unresolved, these emotions can erode the very foundations of our connections with others, leaving us trapped in a cycle of negativity and conflict. Yet, within this complexity, there exists a powerful antidote to anger: forgiveness.

Time to dive into the profound role of forgiveness in resolving anger, explore practical steps toward forgiving and letting go of past grievances, and illuminate the transformative stories of individuals whose embrace of forgiveness has breathed new life into their relationships.

The Role of Forgiveness in Resolving Anger

Forgiveness is often misunderstood as a weakness or a concession, but in reality, it is an act of strength, resilience, and emotional intelligence. The process of releasing anger, resentment, and desire for revenge can hold us captive, allowing us to move forward with greater clarity and peace. Here's why forgiveness is pivotal in resolving anger:

1. <u>Emotional Liberation</u>: Forgiveness is a path to emotional liberation. By forgiving, you free yourself from the heavy burden of anger and resentment. It's like unshackling yourself from the chains that bind you to past hurts.

2. <u>Healing Relationships</u>: Forgiveness has the power to heal wounded relationships. It opens the door to communication and reconciliation, allowing both parties to grow and mend the rift.

3. <u>Personal Growth</u>: Embracing forgiveness fosters personal growth. It requires self-reflection, empathy, and a willingness to let go of grudges. Through forgiveness, you develop emotional resilience and maturity.

4. <u>Reduced Stress</u>: Unresolved anger and resentment can lead to chronic stress, impacting your physical and emotional well-being. Forgiveness is a way to reduce this stress and its negative effects.

5. <u>Empowerment</u>: Forgiveness is an empowering choice. It allows you to take control of your emotional responses and reactions. It's a declaration that you refuse to be defined by your past pain.

Steps Toward Forgiveness and Letting Go

While forgiveness is a noble goal, it's not always an easy journey. Here are some practical steps to help you embark on the path of forgiveness:

1. <u>Acknowledge Your Anger</u>: Start by acknowledging your anger and the pain it represents. Understand that feeling angry is normal when you've been hurt or wronged.

2. <u>Understand the Benefits</u>: Reflect on the benefits of forgiveness. Consider how it can free you from the burden of anger, improve your relationships, and enhance your overall well-being.

3. <u>Practice Empathy</u>: Try to see the situation from the other person's perspective. This doesn't mean condoning their actions but gaining insight into their motivations and emotions.

4. <u>Let Go of the Past</u>: Recognize that holding onto past grievances only prolongs your suffering. Decide to let go of the past and its power over your present.

5. <u>Express Your Feelings</u>: Communicate your feelings to the person who has hurt you, if appropriate and safe to do so. Expressing your emotions can be a step toward resolution.

6. <u>Seek Support</u>: Forgiveness can be challenging, and you don't have to go through it alone. Seek support from friends, family, or a therapist who can provide guidance and a listening ear.

Stories of Forgiveness and Transformation

Forgiveness can transform individuals and entire relationships. Here are a few real-life stories of how forgiveness has changed the course of these relationships:

1. <u>Reuniting Siblings</u>: Sarah and David were estranged siblings who hadn't spoken for years due to a bitter feud over their parents' inheritance. After a family tragedy, they decided to put aside their anger

and reach out to each other. Through heartfelt conversations and mutual forgiveness, they rebuilt their relationship and now support each other in times of need.

2. <u>Healing a Marriage</u>: Emily and Mark had been married for over a decade but had grown distant due to unresolved conflicts and resentment. They decided to attend couples therapy and learned the art of forgiveness. By forgiving each other for past mistakes and committing to communicate openly, their marriage underwent a remarkable transformation, becoming stronger and more loving than ever.

3. <u>Reconnecting with a Friend</u>: Alex and Mia had been best friends since childhood, but a betrayal had torn their friendship apart. Years later, Alex reached out to Mia with a heartfelt letter expressing his remorse and forgiveness. Deeply moved, Mia decided to let go of her anger and reconnect with her old friend. Their renewed bond was stronger and more genuine than before.

Forgiveness is a profound and healing force that can mend fractured relationships and release us from the grip of anger and resentment. By understanding its role in resolving anger, taking deliberate steps toward forgiveness, and drawing inspiration from stories of transformation, you can harness the power of forgiveness to create healthier, more harmonious relationships in your life. It is not a sign of weakness but a testament to your inner strength and capacity for growth.

Building a Culture of Appreciation

In the intricate dance of human relationships, there exists a powerful elixir that can transform the emotional climate, nurture connection, and mitigate the destructive force of anger: appreciation. It is the art of recognizing and valuing the qualities, actions, and contributions of those we hold dear. Here, we will explore the profound importance of appreciation and positive reinforcement, provide practical exercises to cultivate gratitude and appreciation in your relationships and share inspiring examples of how appreciation can shape the emotional landscape of your connections.

The Importance of Appreciation and Positive Reinforcement

Appreciation is the foundation for healthy and fulfilling relationships. It serves as a catalyst for nurturing connection, fostering trust, and promoting emotional well-being. Here are some key reasons why appreciation and positive reinforcement are indispensable in relationships:

1. <u>Strengthening Bonds</u>: When you express appreciation, you acknowledge the value and significance of the people in your life. This strengthens the bonds of trust and intimacy, creating a deeper connection.

2. <u>Boosting Self-Esteem</u>: Positive reinforcement and appreciation boost self-esteem and self-worth for both the recipient and the giver. It fosters a sense of being valued and respected.

3. <u>Enhancing Communication</u>: Expressing appreciation encourages open and effective communication. It creates a safe space for sharing thoughts and feelings, reducing the likelihood of miscommunication and conflict.

4. <u>Mitigating Anger and Resentment</u>: People who feel appreciated are less likely to harbor anger and resentment. Appreciation can diffuse potential anger triggers and promote forgiveness.

5. <u>Encouraging Positive Behavior</u>: Positive reinforcement can encourage and reinforce positive behavior. When people feel their efforts are recognized and appreciated, they are motivated to continue those behaviors.

Exercises for Cultivating Gratitude and Appreciation in Relationships

Cultivating a culture of appreciation in your relationships is a deliberate practice that requires effort and intention. Here are some exercises to help you develop gratitude and appreciation in your interactions with others:

1. <u>Daily Gratitude Journal</u>: Take a few moments each day to jot down things you appreciate about the people in your life. This simple practice can shift your focus toward positivity.

2. <u>Express Appreciation</u>: Make it a habit to express appreciation verbally or through written notes. Let the people around you know that you value and appreciate them.

3. <u>Active Listening</u>: Practice active listening when engaging in conversations. Show genuine interest in what others say, and respond with empathy and appreciation for their perspective.

4. <u>Appreciation Circle</u>: Create an appreciation circle within your family or friend group. Gather regularly to express gratitude and appreciation for one another's qualities and actions.

5. <u>Random Acts of Kindness</u>: Surprise your loved ones with unexpected acts of kindness and appreciation. It could be as simple as preparing their favorite meal or leaving a heartfelt note.

Examples of Appreciation Transforming Relationships

The power of appreciation to transform the emotional climate of a relationship is evident in countless real-life stories:

1. A Marriage Revived: Sarah and John had been married for years, and over time, they had drifted apart due to the demands of their busy lives. One day, John began a habit of leaving little notes of appreciation for Sarah, expressing his gratitude for the small things she did. Sarah, in turn, started to reciprocate. Their newfound appreciation for each other's efforts rekindled the spark in their marriage, and they found themselves more connected than ever before.

2. Rebuilding Trust: Emily had a strained relationship with her teenage daughter, Lily, after a period of miscommunication and conflict. To bridge the gap, Emily initiated regular conversations where she expressed appreciation for Lily's unique qualities and efforts. This simple act of recognition and appreciation helped rebuild trust between them and paved the way for healthier communication.

3. A Positive Work Environment: Mark, a manager at a tech company, noticed tension and frustration among his team members. To address this, he began a practice of publicly recognizing and appreciating the contributions of each team member during weekly meetings. The atmosphere in the workplace shifted dramatically as employees felt valued and motivated to collaborate more effectively.

Appreciation is a potent force that can transform the emotional landscape of your relationships. By understanding its significance, practicing gratitude and appreciation, and drawing inspiration from stories of transformation, you can cultivate a culture of appreciation that nurtures connection, fosters trust, and mitigates anger in your relationships. It is a gift that keeps on giving, enriching the lives of both givers and recipients alike, and creating a harmonious and loving environment for all.

Chapter Nine
Long-Term Strategies for Anger Management

As we navigate the labyrinthine journey of life, we often encounter challenges that stir our emotions, particularly the turbulent tempest known as anger. It's a feeling we've all grappled with at one time or another, whether as a fleeting flicker or an overwhelming inferno. But, dear reader, if you've journeyed with me through the pages of this book, you've come to understand that anger need not be an uncontrollable force wreaking havoc on your life and relationships. There is hope; within these pages, you'll find the keys to long-term anger management strategies.

Now, allow me to share a personal story of how I discovered the profound significance of long-term anger management strategies and why I've included this chapter in our book.

Years ago, I was entangled in an inescapable web of anger. The triggers were many—a demanding job, financial pressures, and personal relationships riddled with conflict. My anger was like a shadow, always lurking, waiting for the slightest provocation to rear its head. It affected my health, my relationships, and my overall well-being.

One day, as I was engulfed in a fit of rage, I realized the magnitude of the damage it was causing. It was as if I had been living my life in a turbulent storm, unable to see the beauty of the clear skies beyond. In that moment of clarity, I made a commitment to change—to find a way out of the storm and into the sunlight of serenity.

This chapter exists because I understand the challenges of managing anger and believe in long-term strategies' transformative power. It's not just about controlling anger in the heat of the moment; it's about reshaping your relationship with anger, forging a path toward lasting change, and reclaiming the peace and joy that anger often steals from us.

Now, you might be wondering why you should invest your time delving into long-term anger management strategies. Here's what you stand to gain from this chapter's insights and guidance:

1. Lasting Change: You'll discover how to enact profound and lasting changes in your relationship with anger. These are not quick fixes but strategies that can transform your life over the long haul.

2. Improved Health: Long-term anger management strategies can positively impact your physical and mental health. You'll learn how to reduce stress, lower blood pressure, and boost your overall well-being.

3. Strengthened Relationships: Mastering long-term strategies will foster healthier, more harmonious relationships. Anger will no longer be the destructive force that drives people away; instead, it will become a catalyst for growth and understanding.

4. Enhanced Emotional Resilience: Long-term strategies equip you with the tools to weather life's storms with grace and resilience. You'll find yourself better prepared to handle adversity and navigate challenges.

5. Personal Growth: As you embark on the journey of long-term anger management, you'll discover aspects of yourself you never knew existed. It's a path of self-discovery and growth that can lead to a more fulfilling life.

So, dear reader, if you've come this far, know that you're on the verge of a transformational journey. In the following pages, you'll uncover a treasure trove of strategies, exercises, and insights to help you master the art of managing anger over the long term. It's time to step out of the storm and into the sunshine of serenity.

Monitoring and Maintaining Progress

As you embark on the journey of long-term anger management, it's important to recognize that change is not a one-time event but a continuous process. Just as a ship needs a compass to navigate the open sea, you, too, require a reliable tool to steer your course toward lasting anger management. This is your compass, guiding you toward self-assessment, progress tracking, and the rewarding journey of sustained change.

The Importance of Ongoing Self-Assessment

Imagine you're on a road trip to a distant destination. You wouldn't simply set your GPS once and forget about it. No, you'd regularly check your progress, ensure you're on the right path, and make necessary adjustments. Similarly, ongoing self-assessment is your compass for success in the anger management journey.

Reflection and Self-Awareness: Self-assessment begins with honest reflection. Take time regularly to ponder your thoughts, emotions, and actions. What triggers your anger? How do you respond to it? Have you noticed patterns or trends in your behavior since starting your anger management journey? By developing self-awareness, you can identify areas that need improvement.

Monitoring Triggers: Keep a journal to track anger triggers. Note the situations, people, or circumstances that tend to provoke your anger. Understanding your triggers allows you to anticipate them and develop strategies for coping effectively.

Emotional Check-Ins: Periodically check in with yourself emotionally. Use a scale from 1 to 10 to rate your anger levels. Are you experiencing more calm and less anger than before? Tracking your emotional state over time can help you visualize your progress.

Feedback from Others: Don't underestimate the power of feedback from those close to you. Trusted friends or family members may provide valuable insights into your anger management journey. Be open to their observations and constructive criticism.

Tools for Tracking Progress in Anger Management

Progress tracking is like charting your journey on a map. It helps you see how far you've come and how much further you need to go. Here are some tools and techniques to aid you in tracking your progress:

Goal Setting: Clearly define your anger management goals, both short-term and long-term. Make them specific, measurable, achievable, relevant, and time-bound (SMART). Regularly assess your progress toward these goals.

Daily or Weekly Journals: Maintain a journal to record your thoughts, emotions, and reactions. Include instances where you successfully managed anger, as well as those where you struggled. Reflect on what worked and what didn't.

Self-Assessment Questionnaires: Utilize self-assessment questionnaires and quizzes related to anger management. These can help you objectively measure your progress and identify areas requiring further attention.

Technology-Assisted Tracking: Numerous apps and digital tools are designed to track emotions and behaviors. Some of these tools can provide graphs and visualizations of your progress, making it easier to see trends.

Milestone Celebrations: Celebrate your achievements along the way. Recognize and reward yourself for reaching milestones in your anger management journey. Positive reinforcement can motivate continued progress.

Success Stories of Long-Term Anger Management

To illustrate the importance of ongoing self-assessment and progress tracking, let's delve into some success stories of individuals who have embraced these practices in their long-term anger management journeys:

Case Study 1: Sarah's Journey

Sarah, a marketing executive, struggled with anger issues that affected her professional relationships. She began her anger management journey by diligently tracking her anger triggers, responses, and progress in a journal. Over time, she identified patterns and gradually developed healthier coping strategies. Sarah's self-assessment and tracking allowed her to transform her approach to anger, leading to improved relationships and career growth.

Case Study 2: David's Turning Point

David, a high school teacher, was overwhelmed by anger in the classroom, leading to strained relationships with students and colleagues. Recognizing the need for change, he set specific goals for his anger management journey and began tracking his daily emotions and reactions. Through ongoing reflection, David noticed that deep breathing exercises helped him diffuse anger. By monitoring his progress and adjusting his techniques, he transformed his classroom environment and became an influential mentor to his students.

Case Study 3: Elena's Remarkable Transformation

Elena's anger issues were deeply rooted in her personal life, affecting her family dynamics. She committed to weekly self-assessment through journaling and used emotion-tracking apps to monitor her progress. As the months passed, Elena's insights from self-assessment led to significant changes. She recognized the importance of setting boundaries, practicing mindfulness, and seeking support from loved ones. Her journey demonstrates how consistent self-assessment can lead to lasting transformation in personal relationships.

Monitoring and maintaining progress in your long-term anger management journey is beneficial and essential. Just as a skilled navigator continually checks their course, you must regularly assess your path to ensure you're headed in the right direction. With self-awareness, goal setting, and the tools to track your progress, you can confidently navigate toward a future filled with emotional balance and lasting anger management success.

When to Seek Professional Help

Throughout your anger management journey, there may come a time when you realize that your efforts, while commendable, may not be enough to address the complexity of your anger issues. This is a pivotal moment that requires the wisdom to recognize when seeking professional help is not only advisable but essential. We will explore the guidelines for recognizing when professional assistance is necessary, the numerous benefits of therapy or counseling for anger management, and where to find the help you need.

Guidelines for Recognizing When to Seek Professional Assistance

Chronic Anger: If you find that anger has become a chronic and unrelenting part of your life, persisting for weeks, months, or even years, it's time to consider professional help. Chronic anger can take a toll on your physical and mental health, as well as your relationships.

Escalation of Anger: When your anger escalates to the point of causing harm to yourself or others, it's a clear sign that professional intervention is necessary. This harm can be physical, emotional, or psychological and should not be taken lightly.

Inability to Control Anger: Despite your best efforts, if you find it nearly impossible to control your anger or apply the anger management techniques you've learned, it strongly indicates that you need professional guidance.

Interference with Daily Life: When anger interferes with your daily life, affecting your work, relationships, and overall well-being, it's time to seek help. This interference may manifest as frequent conflicts, damaged relationships, or even job loss.

Physical Symptoms: If your anger is accompanied by physical symptoms such as elevated blood pressure, headaches, digestive problems, or other health issues, these can be warning signs that it's time to consult a professional.

Substance Abuse: If you turn to alcohol, drugs, or other substances as a way to cope with anger, this is a red flag. Substance abuse and anger often go hand in hand, and addressing one may require addressing the other.

Isolation: Social withdrawal and isolation are common responses to unmanaged anger. If you find yourself increasingly isolated from friends and loved ones due to anger issues, it's crucial to seek help.

The Benefits of Therapy or Counseling for Anger Management

Seeking professional help for anger management can be transformative and highly beneficial. Here are some of the advantages:

Expert Guidance: Mental health professionals, such as therapists, counselors, or psychologists, possess specialized knowledge and experience in helping individuals manage their anger effectively.

Personalized Approach: Professionals can tailor their approach to your unique needs, addressing the underlying causes of your anger and providing personalized strategies for improvement.

Safe Environment: Therapy or counseling offers a safe, confidential space to express your thoughts and emotions without judgment. This can encourage self-reflection and healing.

Effective Techniques: Professionals can teach you evidence-based techniques and coping strategies that have been proven to work in anger management. These techniques are often more effective than self-help methods alone.

Emotional Support: Therapists and counselors offer emotional support and empathy, helping you explore the emotional root of your anger and guiding you toward healthier responses.

Conflict Resolution: They can assist in improving communication skills, conflict resolution, and assertiveness, which are essential for healthier relationships.

Preventing Relapse: Professionals can help you identify potential relapse triggers and provide tools to prevent a return to destructive anger patterns.

Resources for Finding Professional Help

Primary Care Physician: Start by consulting your primary care physician. They can provide referrals to mental health professionals who specialize in anger management.

Mental Health Associations: Organizations like the American Psychological Association (APA) and the National Association of Social Workers (NASW) have directories to help you find qualified professionals in your area.

Online Directories: Numerous online directories allow you to search for therapists, counselors, or psychologists based on your location and specific needs. Psychology Today and GoodTherapy are excellent resources.

Employee Assistance Programs (EAP): Many employers offer EAPs that provide confidential counseling services to employees and their families. Check with your HR department for details.

Community Mental Health Centers: Local mental health centers often provide affordable counseling services. You can contact them directly or seek referrals from your physician.

Insurance Providers: If you have health insurance, check with your insurance provider for a list of in-network mental health professionals.

Word of Mouth: Seek recommendations from friends, family members, or support groups who may have had positive experiences with mental health professionals.

In conclusion, recognizing when to seek professional help for anger management is a courageous step toward improving your well-being and relationships. Don't hesitate to reach out to a qualified therapist or counselor who can provide the expertise, guidance, and support needed to navigate the complexities of anger and its underlying causes. In doing so, you can look forward to a healthier, more balanced, and happier life.

Joining Support Groups

Anger management can often feel like a solitary journey, but it doesn't have to be. While individual therapy or counseling can be highly effective, there's another valuable resource that should not be overlooked: support groups. I want to show you the benefits of joining anger management support groups, provide guidance on how to find and join the right group and share testimonials from individuals who have found solace, understanding, and growth within these groups.

Benefits of Joining Anger Management Support Groups

Shared Experiences: Support groups offer a unique opportunity to connect with others who are facing similar anger challenges. Sharing your experiences and hearing others' stories can create a sense of belonging and reduce feelings of isolation.

Peer Empathy: Members of support groups understand the struggles you're going through because they've been there themselves. This empathy from peers can be incredibly comforting and validating.

Non-Judgmental Environment: Support groups provide a safe, non-judgmental space where you can openly discuss your anger issues, fears, and frustrations without the fear of being criticized.

Accountability: Group members often hold each other accountable for their actions and progress. Knowing that you have a supportive community to answer to can be a motivating factor in managing anger.

Learning Opportunities: These groups are a valuable source of knowledge and coping strategies. Members often share practical tips, techniques, and resources that have helped them in their journey toward anger management.

Constructive Feedback: Hearing feedback and insights from others can provide you with different perspectives on your own behavior and help you identify areas for improvement.

Improved Communication: Support groups often focus on improving communication skills, which can be incredibly beneficial for resolving conflicts in personal and professional relationships.

Finding and Joining the Right Group

Online Research: Start your search online. Many support groups have websites or listings on social media platforms. You can use search engines, social media groups, and forums dedicated to anger management to find options that match your needs.

Therapist or Counselor Recommendations: If you are already working with a therapist or counselor, they may be able to recommend suitable support groups in your area or online.

Community Centers and Mental Health Organizations: Local community centers and mental health organizations often host support groups. Contact them directly or check their websites for information.

Ask Your Healthcare Provider: If you're under the care of a healthcare provider for any physical or mental health issue, inquire about support groups. They may have valuable insights or referrals.

Word of Mouth: Seek recommendations from friends, family members, or colleagues who may have had positive experiences with support groups or know someone who has.

Online Support Groups: If in-person meetings aren't an option or you prefer the anonymity of online interaction, consider joining virtual support groups. Websites and platforms like Meetup, Reddit, and Facebook have groups dedicated to anger management.

Testimonials from Support Group Members

Sarah's Story: Sarah had struggled with anger for most of her life, often leading to heated arguments and damaged relationships. She decided to join a local anger management support group after a particularly explosive argument with her spouse. Within the group, Sarah found solace in knowing she wasn't alone in her struggles. "Hearing others share their experiences was incredibly validating," she says. "I felt understood and accepted in a way I hadn't before. Over time, I learned effective strategies for managing my anger and maintaining healthier relationships."

John's Journey: John was initially hesitant to join a support group, fearing that it would be a sign of weakness. However, his therapist recommended it, emphasizing the sense of community and the potential for personal growth. John's experience was transformative. "The group became like a second family," he explains. "We held each other accountable, celebrated our victories, and supported each other through setbacks. It was a game-changer in my journey toward anger management."

Lisa's Lifeline: Lisa had been struggling with anger in her workplace, leading to strained professional relationships and potential career setbacks. She found an online anger management support group and was surprised by the immediate impact. "I learned practical strategies for managing my anger at work and communicating more effectively," Lisa shares. "I'm now in a much better place professionally, and I owe a large part of that to the support group."

Support groups are an invaluable resource on your path to anger management. They offer understanding, empathy, and guidance from individuals who have faced similar challenges. By sharing experiences, coping strategies, and learning opportunities, these groups can significantly enhance your journey toward a healthier, more balanced life. Whether you opt for in-person or online support groups, the connections you make and the knowledge you gain can be instrumental in your long-term success.

Continuing Education on Anger Management

Anger management is not a one-time endeavor but a lifelong journey toward self-improvement and emotional well-being. As you progress on this path, it's essential to continue educating yourself and staying updated with the latest developments in anger management. Be encouraged to continue learning and growth in the field of anger management, offer recommendations for books, courses, and workshops, and share the latest research and developments in anger management strategies.

The Importance of Ongoing Learning

Anger management, like any other skill, benefits from continuous learning and refinement. Here are a few reasons why ongoing education is crucial:

Deepening Understanding: As you delve deeper into the subject, you gain a more profound understanding of the underlying causes of anger and various effective strategies for managing it.

Staying Motivated: Learning new techniques and approaches can motivate you to work on anger issues. It prevents complacency and encourages personal growth.

Adapting to Change: The world is constantly evolving, and so are our stressors and triggers. Staying updated allows you to adapt your anger management strategies to new challenges.

Offering Support: By educating yourself further, you can also become a valuable source of knowledge and support for others who are on a similar journey.

Recommended Resources for Ongoing Learning

Books on Anger Management:

The Anger Workbook by Les Carter and Frank Minirth offers practical exercises and strategies for managing anger effectively.

Anger: Wisdom for Cooling the Flames by Thich Nhat Hanh: A book that combines mindfulness and meditation practices to help you transform anger into understanding and compassion.

Online Courses:

Coursera: Offers courses like "Managing Your Health: The Role of Physical Therapy and Exercise" and "Managing the Company of Snakes: Understanding and Managing Emotions at Work."

Udemy: Provides various anger management courses, including "Anger Management: Understanding Anger and Learning to Cope."

Workshops and Seminars:

Check with local community centers, mental health organizations, and anger management therapists for workshops and seminars in your area.

Therapy and Counseling:

Consider continuing therapy or counseling sessions, even if you've made significant progress. These sessions provide a consistent space for growth and self-reflection.

Research Articles and Journals:

Explore academic journals and publications on psychology and anger management to stay informed about the latest research findings and evidence-based practices.

The Latest Developments in Anger Management

The field of anger management is continuously evolving, with researchers and professionals exploring new approaches and refining existing strategies. Some recent developments include:

Neuroscientific Insights: Advances in neuroscience have provided valuable insights into how the brain processes anger and emotions.

These findings can inform more effective anger management techniques.

Virtual Reality Therapy: Virtual reality (VR) therapy is emerging as a promising tool for anger management. VR environments can help individuals practice anger management skills in realistic scenarios.

Online Apps and Resources: There's a growing market for mobile apps and online resources designed to help individuals manage anger. These tools often incorporate mindfulness, cognitive-behavioral therapy, and relaxation techniques.

Cultural Sensitivity: Anger management approaches are becoming more culturally sensitive, recognizing that different cultural backgrounds may influence how anger is expressed and managed.

Mindfulness-Based Approaches: Mindfulness techniques, such as meditation and deep breathing exercises, continue to gain popularity as effective anger management tools. Research is ongoing to understand their impact better.

Your journey toward effective anger management doesn't end when you achieve initial success. It's a lifelong process that can benefit from ongoing education and self-improvement. By staying informed about the latest developments, exploring new resources, and deepening your understanding of anger management, you can continue to grow and maintain emotional well-being. Embrace the opportunity for lifelong learning, and you'll be better equipped to face any challenges that come your way.

Paying It Forward

As you progress on your journey towards effective anger management and healthier relationships, you may find that sharing your knowledge and experiences with others becomes a way of giving back and a powerful tool for reinforcing your progress. Moving forward, we'll explore the concept of "paying it forward," inspire you to share your knowledge and support others, offer suggestions for community involvement and advocacy, and share stories of how teaching others can enhance your personal growth and reinforce your commitment to anger management.

The Power of Sharing Knowledge

Sharing your knowledge and experiences with others is a transformative act, both for the giver and the receiver. Here's why paying it forward is so valuable:

Reinforces Your Understanding: Teaching others forces you to articulate and explain concepts, which deepens your understanding and mastery of anger management techniques.

Creates a Supportive Community: Helping others on their journey creates a supportive and empathetic community of individuals working towards similar goals.

Inspires Accountability: Guiding and supporting others reinforces your commitment to anger management and emotional well-being.

Fosters Empathy: Hearing about others' struggles and successes can enhance your empathy and emotional intelligence, essential for managing anger effectively.

Ways to Pay It Forward

Here are some ways to pay it forward and make a positive impact: Mentorship: Offer to mentor someone just beginning their journey in anger management. Share your insights, techniques, and strategies for success.

Support Groups: Join or create a local or online support group where individuals can share their experiences, challenges, and triumphs in managing anger.

Advocacy: Become an advocate for anger management awareness. Encourage your community to recognize the importance of emotional well-being and support initiatives related to mental health.

Volunteer: Consider volunteering your time and skills to organizations focusing on anger management, mental health, or community well-being. You can lead workshops or participate in community outreach.

Online Communities: Participate in online forums, social media groups, or platforms where individuals seek advice and support for anger management. Offer your guidance and encouragement.

Community Involvement and Advocacy

Engaging with your community and advocating for better anger management practices can have a far-reaching impact. Here's how you can get involved:

Local Workshops: Organize or participate in local workshops on anger management and emotional well-being. These events can reach individuals who may not have easy access to resources.

School Programs: Collaborate with schools to introduce anger management programs for students. Teaching emotional regulation skills early can have a long-lasting effect.

Employee Assistance Programs (EAPs): Advocate for improved EAPs in workplaces. Many people experience stress and anger at work, and accessible resources can make a significant difference.

Public Awareness Campaigns: Work with local mental health organizations to launch public awareness campaigns about anger management and mental health. Education can reduce stigma and encourage seeking help.

Stories of Impact

Let's explore stories of individuals who paid it forward and, in doing so, strengthened their commitment to anger management.

John's Story: John struggled with anger issues for most of his life. After years of therapy and self-improvement, he decided to start an anger management support group in his community. As he shared his experiences and strategies with others, he found that teaching reinforced his commitment to managing anger constructively. Witnessing group members' progress further motivated him to continue his own growth.

Lena's Story: Lena had a challenging childhood filled with anger and conflict. She decided to become a school counselor and implemented an anger management program in her school. As she taught students how to recognize and manage their anger, she found her emotional intelligence improving. Seeing the positive impact on her students encouraged her to maintain her anger management practices.

<u>David's Story</u>: David, a successful businessman, experienced anger-related issues at work. He began volunteering at a local nonprofit organization that provided anger management resources to underserved communities. He became more patient and understanding as he led workshops and shared his expertise. The act of teaching others transformed his approach to anger management.

Paying it forward through teaching, mentoring, and community involvement can be a fulfilling and enriching aspect of your anger management journey. By sharing your knowledge and experiences, you support others in their growth and reinforce your commitment to managing anger effectively. As you inspire change in the lives of those around you, you'll find that your progress becomes even more profound and lasting.

Chapter Ten
CONCLUSION

As I sit here, reflecting on the journey we've embarked upon together through the pages of this book, my mind is drawn to a memory, a pivotal moment that propelled me to write these words. It's a memory that still stirs a sense of purpose and echoes the essence of why I penned this book on anger management.

Several years ago, I was in a situation where anger gripped me like a vise. It was during a family gathering when laughter, love, and shared stories should have prevailed. But, alas, the dark cloud of anger overshadowed the day.

I had allowed anger to rob me of a beautiful moment, and I watched helplessly as it cast its shadow over the faces of my loved ones. It was a stark reminder of the corrosive nature of unmanaged anger and how it can seep into the most cherished aspects of our lives, wreaking havoc where joy should reside.

That day, I made a promise to myself that echoed through the years and inspired the creation of this book. I vowed not only to confront my own anger but also to offer guidance and support to others seeking the same transformation. And so, with that memory etched in my heart, I embarked on a journey of self-discovery and exploration.

Throughout these pages, we've unraveled the intricate threads of anger, explored its physiological and psychological dimensions, debunked myths, and embraced a holistic approach to anger management. We've practiced mindfulness and relaxation techniques, embraced cognitive behavioral strategies, nurtured emotional intelligence, and fine-tuned our lifestyles.

We've learned to identify our anger triggers, set healthy boundaries, and understand the power of forgiveness and appreciation. We've discovered that this journey is not just about managing anger; it's about rewiring our emotional responses, deepening our relationships, and, ultimately, transforming ourselves into more resilient, empathetic, and balanced individuals.

As you reach the end of this book, I encourage you to remember that anger management is not a destination but a lifelong journey. The insights and techniques you've gained here are powerful tools that require practice and patience. Embrace them as part of your daily life, and allow them to guide you toward lasting change.

The benefits of effective anger management are profound. Improved relationships, enhanced emotional well-being, and greater control over your life await you. But more than that, you'll discover a deeper connection with yourself and those around you, a connection rooted in empathy, understanding, and love.

As you continue your journey toward effective anger management, I offer my sincerest well wishes. May you find the calmness within, may your relationships flourish, and may your life be filled with the joy and serenity that come from embracing emotional freedom.

Remember, you have the power to transform anger into calmness, and I believe in your capacity to do so. Your journey doesn't end here; it's just beginning. Embrace it with an open heart, and may your path be paved with serenity, empathy, and enduring happiness.

Thank you for taking this journey with me.

www.ingramcontent.com/pod-product-compliance
Lightning Source LLC
LaVergne TN
LVHW021823060526
838201LV00058B/3485